The Possible

The Possible Is Monstrous

Selected Poems by
Friedrich Dürrenmatt

Translated by
Daniele Pantano

Black Lawrence Press
New York

Black Lawrence Press
www.blacklawrence.com

Executive Editor: Diane Goettel
Book Layout: Steven Seighman

Black Lawrence Press
8405 Bay Parkway C8
Brooklyn, N.Y. 11214
U.S.A.

Published 2010 by Black Lawrence Press, an imprint of Dzanc Books

ISBN: 9780982622810

First edition 2010

Printed in the United States

CENTRE DÜRRENMATT
NEUCHÂTEL

For Nicole

—D.P.

CONTENTS

TRANSLATOR'S NOTE

Friedrich Dürrenmatt (1921–1990) is considered not only the most prominent author of Swiss literature following the Second World War but also one of the most important literary figures of the second half of the twentieth century, rivaled, some scholars argue, only by Beckett, Brecht, Camus, and Sartre. As an author and dramatist, Dürrenmatt is certainly well known in the United States and throughout the world—as a poet, however, he is not. What only a few readers and scholars realize is that in addition to being a prolific writer of prose, Dürrenmatt was also a formidable poet.

Like his Austrian contemporary Thomas Bernhard, whose first literary hero was his grandfather, Dürrenmatt looked up to his grandfather Ulrich Dürrenmatt (1849–1908), a politician, newspaper editor, satirist, and poet, who wrote and published over 2500 poems. In "Mondfinsternis" (1981), Dürrenmatt describes him as "a strange, solitary, and headstrong rebel" and confesses to his envy of one of "Ueli's" achievements in particular: "My grandfather was once sent to prison for ten days because of a poem he wrote. I haven't been honored in that way yet." In 1946, at the end of an unsuccessful tenure as a university student, the young Friedrich, who had adapted a persona similar to his grandfather's, decided to dedicate his life to writing. In fact, he had already begun writing short stories and plays, as well as poems, as early as 1942.

There is naturally a long list of authors who either started their careers as poets or whose writing of poetry receives little notice. Norman Mailer, for example, long harbored the secret wish to "be a vast success at the bar of poetry." In the preface to *Modest Gifts* (2003), Mailer reminds us that his poems simply "offer the reader an easy pleasure," nothing more. At the same time, Mailer admits that he is not "being altogether candid" and hints at the possibility that his poems represent his "embers," his purest work. For Dürrenmatt, poetry is not quite the same aside as it is for the American. He comes from that tradition of the *feuilleton*, the literary pages of those newspapers pored over in

Europe's cafés, where a poem need only appear in such a format. Indeed, one could say the book is the sideshow. Thus Dürrenmatt the poet is as sharp, gutsy, and controversial as Dürrenmatt the author and playwright; his poems are concentrated instances that at first may appear to be meant solely for pleasure but inevitably expose, via their purity, his fundamental *Weltanschauung* that lies at the core of all of his creative endeavors.

It is inherently difficult, if not impossible, to pin down a definitive poetics or thematic landscape in Dürrenmatt's work as a poet. He moves effortlessly from epic ballads, nursery rhymes, and exotic forms such as the *maqam*, to short lyric bursts and personal anecdotes, from socioeconomic critiques of Switzerland and postwar Europe, reinterpretations of ancient myths, and poems about craft, to investigations of modern science and culture. If anything, much like his novels, plays, and even essays (Brian Evenson, in *Selected Writings* [2006], sees him as "one of the few real innovators of the essayistic form"), his poetry continuously questions the possibility of language to represent, in a coherent and authentic manner, modern experience and reality. Yet, while Dürrenmatt was always keen to create a certain linguistic and stylistic distance between text and reader, in his poetry, this distance seems significantly smaller, more intimate. Most of the poems in this volume should be read as lyric confessions in which our author is at his most sincere and humane. The Dürrenmatt scholar and biographer Peter Rüedi, who wrote the afterword for the poems in the original edition—included in the present volume—argues that some of the author's verses offer "rare moments of another, lyric Dürrenmatt," poems "where Dürrenmatt speaks as Dürrenmatt, a voice we can usually hear only in his later prose—pieces where he allows himself some sensitivity." More significantly, often viewed as mere byproducts of his prose, Dürrenmatt's poems, first written on maps, envelopes, napkins, and odd scraps of paper, undoubtedly represent a crucial narrative that parallels, informs, and illuminates his development as an author and playwright.

In 1993 Diogenes Verlag published *Das Mögliche ist ungeheuer* (*The Possible Is Monstrous*), the first individual collection of Dürrenmatt's work as a poet. Surprisingly, this important part of Dürrenmatt's oeuvre has—until now—never been made available to English-speaking readers, except for several of my individual

translations that have appeared in American and British journals, and "The Minotaur," translated by Joel Agee for the *Selected Writings*. This publication of Dürrenmatt's *Selected Poems* in English translation, therefore, fills a crucial gap for readers and scholars interested in Dürrenmatt's work. And it is my hope that it will give a voice to a hitherto silent part of the author's canon in translation and to show that "For Dürrenmatt, poetry is not an occasion to retreat back into the ivory tower but, aside from novel, novella, essay, and comedy, an additional form with which he attempts to penetrate and endure the world" (from the original dust jacket).

I wish to thank Colleen Ryor and Diane Goettel (my wonderful editors at Black Lawrence Press) for their enthusiasm and encouragement, and the editors of the following journals, in which some of these translations first appeared: *The Adirondack Review*, *ARCH* (Washington University in St. Louis), *The Cortland Review*, *EZRA* (Roger Williams University), and *Shadowtrain* (U.K.). I'm grateful to the English Departments at the University of South Florida, Florida Southern College, and Edge Hill University. My thanks to Janine Perret-Sgualdo and Ulrich Weber at the Centre Dürrenmatt, and Susanne Bauknecht, Bettina Haydon, and Erica Maurer at Diogenes. I'm also very indebted to friends and colleagues for their support: Billy Collins, Jay Hopler, Peter Meinke, Deborah McLeod, Victor Peppard, Nicholas Samaras, Gregory Smith, and Phillip Sipiora. Endless gratitude to James Reidel, whose assistance, advice, and criticism during the evolution of these translations helped this book into the world. Last, and most important, I thank my parents, Giuseppe and Katharina, my brother, Michel, my children, Fiona and Giacomo, and my wife, Nicole, for their unceasing love, support, and inspiration.

Daniele Pantano
Liverpool
September 2009

The Possible Is Monstrous

GOTT UND PÉGUY

Wer ist dieser Mensch, sagt Gott, dieser Péguy
 der mich da zu einem französischen
 Nationalisten machen will?
Was gibt er vor meine Gedanken zu kennen?
 Ist er jemals mein Sekretär gewesen
Dem ich meine Briefe diktierte?

Zwar hat er schöne Verse geschrieben, Gedichte
 die bisweilen sogar ich gern lese.
Und er ist tot, ich habe ihn zu mir genommen.
 Aber diese Zeilen da
Habe ich verworfen. Sie vermodern
 wie sein Leib.
Er soll sie mir nicht in den Mund legen.

Denn ich habe es nicht mehr gern, wenn man
 auf die Völker zu reden kommt.
Sie haben mir alle im Verlaufe der Zeit zuviel
 Blut vergossen
Das ihre Hände rot färbt. Ich will nichts mehr
 von ihnen wissen.

Als ob es nicht genügt, wenn ich jeden Menschen
 einzeln begutachte
Ihn hin und her wende, ob nicht doch noch irgend
 etwas an diesem verpfuschten Ding
 zu gebrauchen sei.

Ohne Blick auf die Etikette, die irgendein
 verdrehter Staat quer über seinen Bauch
 geklebt hat
Auf der Franzose steht, geboren neunzehnhundert-
 zehn als Sohn eines Dramenschreibers und
 einer Hebamme
Auch Deutscher aus Dresden, Hinterindier
 Amerikaner oder Ukrainer
Etiketten, wie wenn es sich um mehr oder weniger
 billige Weinsorten handelte.

GOD AND PÉGUY

Who is this man, says God, this Péguy
    who wants to turn me
    into a French nationalist?
Who's he to pretend to know my thoughts?
    Has he ever been my secretary
Whom I've dictated my letters to?

Though he wrote pretty verses, poems
    even I occasionally enjoy reading.
And he's dead, I took him.
    But these lines here
I tossed out. They rot
    like his body.
He shall not put them in my mouth.

For I no longer want to hear
    talk about the nations.
Over time, they've all wasted
    too much blood
That colors their hands red. I don't want
    to hear anything else about them.

As if it's not enough to examine
    every single man
To turn him back and forth
    searching for something still useful
    on this botched thing.

Without looking at the label
    some contorted nation slapped
    across his belly:
French. Born 1910, son
    of a playwright
    and a midwife
German, from Dresden, too, South-East Indian
    American or Ukrainian
Labels, as if we were dealing with more or less
    cheap kinds of wine.

Meint man denn, ich sei ein Restaurateur, der hin
und wieder
Im Keller die Völker besichtigt wie eingemachte
Konfitüren
Einen Topf nach dem andern, und die Quitten
den Stachelbeeren vorzieht?
Als wenn es nicht allein auf jeden Einzelnen
ankäme
Und wenn sein Urahne Kathedralen erfand
um so schlimmer für den Nachkommen
Wenn er keine mehr findet.

Überhaupt lasse man mich ein wenig mit diesem
Frankreich in Ruhe
Mit diesem Deutschland und England, mit all
diesem ewigen Europa.
Ich bin langsam nicht mehr gut darauf zu sprechen
langsam wird es mir langweilig.

Langsam werden mir die Menschenfresser fast lieber
die da irgendwo im Urwald
Im Streit um ein Kamel mit zwei Höckern oder
um einen halbvermoderten Elephantenzahn
Den unnachgiebigen Angehörigen eines fremden
Stammes kurzerhand gar kochen.
Sie beten wenigstens nicht mich an, wie es diese
Europäer vorgeben
Sondern einen Götzen mit sieben Armen und fünf
Beinen
Ein Monstrum, bei dem man nicht weiß, was vorne
ist oder hinten.
Da kann ich doch wenigstens mit gutem Gewissen
diesen armen Schluckern vergeben.

Während diese Franzosen und Schweizer katholische
Aktion betreiben oder reformierte theologische
Zeitschriften herausgeben
Aber nicht den Glauben haben, den ich nun endlich
einmal bei ihnen sehen möchte

Do they think I'm a restaurateur
    who once in a while
Down in the cellar observes the races
    like preserves
One jar after another, and prefers
    quince over gooseberry?
As if it didn't come down
    to every single individual
And if his forefather invented cathedrals
    all the worse for the descendant
If he can no longer find any.

In general one should leave me alone
    with this France
With this Germany and England
    with all this constant Europe.
I don't want to hear about it anymore
    I'm getting bored with it.

I almost prefer the cannibals
    who somewhere in the jungle
Fighting over a camel with two humps
    or a half-rotten tusk
Quickly cook the unyielding member
    of a foreign tribe.
At least they don't pray to me
    like these Europeans pretend to
But an idol with seven arms
    and five legs
A monster, whose front and back
    are indistinguishable.
At least I can in good conscience
    forgive these poor devils.

While these French and Swiss lead
    Catholic campaigns and publish
    reformist and theological magazines
But don't have the faith I finally want
    to see in them

Den Glauben, der Berge versetzt.

Ist irgendwo schon ein schlimmeres Durcheinander
gesehen worden als in diesem Europa?
Solch ein heilloses Kreuz und Quer von Dummheit
und Brutalität, solch ein Wust an unklarem Denken?
Zuerst haben die Spanier gemordet, dann fingen die
Franzosen an
Jedes Volk immer tüchtiger und lustiger als das
andere, mit immer besseren Guillotinen.
Dann die Engländer. Schließlich die Deutschen
und Italiener
Und jetzt, als man schon glaubte, es sei wirklich
einfach nichts mehr anderes möglich als der Friede
Scheint man sich im Osten zu neuen Blutbädern
vorzubereiten.
Ist es ein Wunder, daß mir alle diese europäischen
Völker gleichermaßen verdächtig vorkommen?

Nein, ich habe keinen dieser Morde vergessen
nicht den geringsten und nebensächlichsten
Und keinen General, der sie anordnete, eine
Henry Clay dabei in Brand steckend
Denn ich bin nicht der Gott Frankreichs oder
Deutschlands oder der Sowjetunion
Ich bin ganz und gar nicht ihr Gott, ich bin
nicht der Gott der Sieger––und der Staat
ist immer ein Sieger
Ich bin der Gott derer, die erschlagen am Boden
liegen.

Darum will ich auch nichts mehr von ihren Kreuz-
zügen hören und ihren besten Soldaten
In wessen Namen sie auch kämpfen. Es klingt mir
zu sehr nach Bartholomäusnacht und der
Inquisition.
Charles Péguy schweige davon. Sie stinken mir
zum Himmel.

Was jedoch in diesem jämmerlichen Europa blieb
in dieser ausgebluteten Halbinsel

The faith that moves mountains.

Has there ever been a worse mess
    than in this Europe?
Such a bedeviled crisscross of stupidity
    and brutality, such a jumble of unclear thinking?
First the Spaniards murdered, then
    the French started
Each nation always cleverer and merrier
    than the other, with ever-improving guillotines.
Then the English. Finally the Germans
    and Italians
And now, while nothing but peace
    is imaginable
It seems in the East they are preparing
    for new bloodbaths.
Is it a wonder then that all European nations
    are equally suspicious to me?

No, I have not forgotten any of these murders
    not the slightest or most incidental
And no General who ordered them
    while setting a match to a Henry Clay
For I'm not the God of France or Germany
    or the Soviet Union
I'm not at all their God, I'm not
    the God of victors—and the State
    is always a victor
I'm the God of those who lie
    slain on the ground.

That's why I don't want to hear any more
    about their crusades and best soldiers
In whoever's name they may fight. It sounds
    too much like the St. Bartholomew's Day
    massacre and the Inquisition.
Charles Péguy, be silent of it. They stink
    to high heaven.

But what has remained in this miserable Europe
    in this bloodless peninsula

Die ich zwischen zwei Meere gepreßt habe
  unter dessen Himmel
Immer noch die Völker weiter herumhantieren
  im wackeren Glauben
Ich drücke auf immer und ewig die Augen zu
  sind die Tränen
Und die Gebete, die hin und wieder zwischen
  den Ruinen zu mir hinaufsteigen:
Sie weinen sie alle und in jedem Land beten
  bisweilen einige
Denn die Not ist oft groß. Es ist eine
  Blasphemie, zu sagen
Nur eines der Völker weine ehrbar und
  nur eines
Spreche ehrbare Gebete.

Zum Teufel mit den falschen Meinungen
  die über mich verbreitet werden.

I pressed between two seas
    beneath their heaven
Still, nations continue to fiddle about
    with brave faith
I forever close my eyes to them
    the tears
And prayers that every now and again
    climb through ruins to reach me:
They cry all of them and in every country
    a few pray sometimes
Because the misery is too much.
    It's blasphemous
To say only one nation
    cries decently
Only one speaks decent prayers.

To hell with the wrong opinions
    that are being spread about me.

AN EUROPA

Du ziehst mit leeren Händen
    nach immer purpurenern Horizonten.
    Im Widerschein deiner Feuersbrünste
glüht dir die Stirne noch einmal.

Immer gieriger verschluckt dich die Dämmerung
    die deinem verfehlten Tage folgt.
    Das Gras, das hinter dir aufsteht
tilgt deine Spur.

Nutzlos ist, was Du tust. Deine Pläne
    ein Geschwätz,
    die Stufen zu verkürzen,
die hinab in dein Grab führen, plapperndes Gerippe.

Tor um Tor erschließt dir schweigend die Nacht.
    Ungehört verhallt deine Klage.

Europa!

Wie hast du die Gnade verspielt, die dir schien,
    Wie hast du deinen Mittag vertan!

Die Sonne erhebt sich nun einem anderen Geschlecht,
    das nicht dein Kind ist,
tote Mutter.

TO EUROPE

With empty hands
    you move towards ever-purpling horizons.
    Once more your forehead glows
with your fire's heat in reflection.

Ever greedier it swallows you,
    the Twilight that follows your failed day.
    The grass that rises behind you
blots out your trace.

Your doings are worthless. Your plans
    all talk,
    to shorten the steps
that lead down into your grave, chattering skeleton.

The night silently closes gate after gate on you.
    Your lament fades away, unheard.

Europe!

How you gambled away the mercy that shone for you,
    How you wasted your noon!

Now the sun rises for another race,
    not your child,
dead mother.

WENN ICH DURCH DIE STÄDTE DEUTSCHLANDS GEHE

Wenn ich durch die Städte Deutschlands
 gehe,
bei jedem vierten Schritt mich verirrend

Durch diese schwarzen und grauen Einöden,
 die man
wie riesige Kloakenansammlungen verbrennen
 mußte

Eingeklemmt in die eintönige Masse ihrer
 Bewohner,
ihre Sprache hörend, wissend, daß sie uns
 als Provinzler verachten

Obgleich sie es sind, die in Wahrheit hinter
 dem Mond leben,
die Primusse der Menschheit in jeder nur denkbaren
 Lage

Einst Weltmeister im Dichten und Denken. Schinder
 nicht aus Wildheit
sondern aus Anmaßung, stolz noch auf ihre
 Leiden

Kehre ich erleichtert in mein Land zurück

Und den ganzen Plunder, mit dem ich hier umstellt
 bin
nehme ich wieder auf meine Schultern. Erhobenen
 Hauptes
beginne ich wieder mit Windmühlen zu kämpfen.

Ein ewiger Don Quijote liebe ich mein Land
 indem ich es züchtige
bejahe ich die Welt, indem ich sie verneine

WHEN I WALK THROUGH
GERMAN CITIES

When I walk through German cities,
    getting lost
with every fourth step

Through these black and gray
    wastelands that
like giant cesspits
    had to be burnt down

Stuck in the monotonous mass of its
    denizens,
hearing their language, knowing
    they despise us provincials

Although it is they who are
    behind the times,
mankind's prime in every imaginable
    situation

Once world champions in poetry and thought.
    Oppressors, not out of primitivity
but presumption, proud even
    of their afflictions

Relieved I return to my country

And put all the trash
    that surrounds me here
back onto my shoulders. With my head
    held high I begin again
to fight the windmills.

Always a Don Quixote, I love my country
    by castigating it
affirm the world by negating it

Ein besseres Deutsch redend als die Deutschen.

Speaking a better German than the Germans.

SCHWEIZERPSALM I

Da liegst Du nun, ein Land, lächerlich, mit
zwei, drei Schritten zu durchmessen,
mitten in diesem unglückseligen Kontinent,

genagelt an sein faules Holz, beleckt von der
Flamme seiner Taten.

Die Erde, die Dich trägt, versteint, Hügel auf
Hügel getürmt,
zu einer Landschaft des Monds,
sich an der Ewigkeit brechend, deren Küste
du bist.

O Schweiz! Don Quijote der Völker! Warum muß
ich dich lieben!

Wie oft, in der Verzweiflung, ballte ich bleich
die Faust gegen Dich
entstelltes Antlitz!

Wie ein Maulwurf hütest Du deine Schätze. Es
vermodert, was Du liebst,
und nur, was Du gering achtest, bleibt.

Ich liebe Dich anders, als Du geliebt sein
willst.
Ich bewundere Dich nicht. Ich lasse nicht ab
von Dir,
ein Wolf, der sich in Dich verbiß.

Deine Sattheit mit Füßen stampfend, höhne ich
Dich, wo Du schlecht bist. Deine Ahnen
lassen mich kalt, ich gähne, wenn ich von ihnen
höre.

Nicht das liebe ich, was Du bist, nicht das,
was Du warst,
Aber Deine Möglichkeit liebe ich, die Gnade,

SWISS PSALM I

Here you lie now, a country, ridiculous,
    measured by two, three steps across,
amid this ill-fated continent,

nailed on its rotten timbers, licked
    by the flame of its doings.

The earth that carries you turns into stone,
    hill upon hill,
into a lunar landscape,
breaking itself on eternity, whose coast
    is you.

O Switzerland! Don Quixote of nations! Why
    must I love you!

How often in despair did I shake
    my balled up fist at your
disfigured face!

Like a mole you hoard your treasures.
    What you cherish molders, and only
what you put down remains.

I don't love you the way you want to be
    loved.
You don't give me any awe. I am not
    letting you off so easy,
not this wolf biting you.

Trampling your stuffed belly,
    I jeer your sickness. Your ancestors
leave me cold, I yawn
    when I hear of them.

I don't love what you are,
    don't love what you were,
I love your possibility, the always-bright mercy

die immer hell über dir schwebt,
Das Abenteuer, heute Dir anzugehören, die
Kühnheit,
jetzt, gerade jetzt, keine Furcht zu haben,
den heiligen Wahnsinn, Dich zu bejahen!

Denn mein Land bist Du nur, wenn Du ein Wunder
bist,
ein Mann, der nicht einsinkt, wenn er über das
Meer schreitet.
So dürste ich nach Deinem Glauben, mein Land.

that floats above you,
The adventure of belonging to you, today,
the boldness
to not fear, now, just now,
the holy madness to affirm you!

For you are my country only
when you are a miracle,
a man who doesn't drown
when he walks across water.
So I thirst after your faith, my country.

SCHWEIZERPSALM II

Was zum Teufel soll ich mit diesem Land anfangen?

Es breitet sich, zwei Schritte in die
Länge und drei in die Breite
wie der Garten eines Fabrikanten zu meinen
Füßen aus,
der in undurchsichtigen Geschäften
verreist ist.

Vielleicht wird er in zwanzig oder fünfzig
Jahren bankerott machen,
jammernde Familien zurücklassend und Historiker,
die bestürzt nach Ursachen
forschen.

In den Vereinigten Staaten von Nordamerika
kann man eine ganze Woche im Schnellzug sitzen,
bis man, um einen verwitterten Ausläufer
der Rocky Mountains biegend,
den großen Ozean sieht.

In Rußland ist die Transsibirische Eisenbahn
ein so unermeßliches Unternehmen, daß
ganze Züge
überhaupt nicht angekommen sind, Jahre
lang durch die Wüste Gobi
schnaubend.

Der Himmel ist wirklich sonst überall unendlich
und die Erde
breitet sich überall ohne Grenzen aus.
Ins Meer tauchend erhebt sie sich wieder
anderswo zu neuen Kontinenten.
Reisende haben mir das versichert.

Wenn man jedoch in diesem Land Eisenbahnzug
fährt,
ist man in vier fünf Stunden von einer

SWISS PSALM II

What the devil should I do with this country?

It spreads at my feet, two steps
in length and three
in width, like the garden
of an industrialist
who's out of town
on some shady business.

Maybe in twenty or fifty years
he'll be bankrupt,
leaving behind families wailing
and perplexed historians searching
for explanations.

In the United States of America, one can sit
for an entire week on a fast train
until, curving around a weather-beaten
foothill of the Rocky Mountains,
one sees the great ocean.

In Russia, the Tran-Siberian Express
is such an overwhelming venture
that entire trains,
steaming for years
through the Gobi desert,
never arrived.

Everywhere else the sky is infinite
and the earth
spreads itself limitlessly.
Diving into the sea, it surfaces
somewhere else as a new continent.
Travelers assure me of this.

But when one rides a train
in this country,
one can travel from one border

Grenze zur andern gekommen
und stochert sich im Speisewagen beim
Anblick des Bodensees
die letzten Reste des Menüs aus den
Zähnen,
das man in Genf begonnen hat.

Und dabei hätte man die Distanzen so furchtbar nötig.

Oft, wenn ich zornig bin und ohne Hoffnung
bin, sage ich:
Dieses Land ist ein Scheißland.

Es liegt vor mir sozusagen in den vier Rahmen
meiner Fenster.
Ein Teller mit fetter Speise aus einem
Hause, das einst gute
Zeiten sah, und heute noch bessere.

Vorgesetzt einem Hund, gespendet von einer
alten Dame,
die—davon spricht sie immer—achthundertfünfzig
Jahre ununterbrochen anständig
gelebt hat. Sie sei barmherzig und tierliebend
sagt die Nachbarschaft.

Dennoch mag ich aus diesem Teller nicht fressen.
Aber ich muß,
Auch ein Hund will leben. Die Zeit ist jetzt
schlimm.
Nur merken es noch wenige.—
Und die Berge liebe ich eigentlich auch nicht.

Wie wenn es irgendwie sinnvoll wäre, die Köpfe
und Gräte
in so hohe Höhen zu stecken, wo es immer schneit,
sogar noch im Hochsommer.

Und dann steht man da in Eis gepanzert, ohne
Leben und gemeingefährlich,
daß am Schluß nicht einmal die Gemsen mehr

to the other in four or five
hours and looking at Lake Constance
still pick one's teeth
for the remains
of the meal one sat down to
in Geneva.

And one is in such dire need
of distances at that.

Often, when I'm angry and without hope,
I say:
This country is a land of shit.

It lies before me, in the four frames of my windows,
so to speak.
A plate with a fat dish from a once
prosperous house
that's even more so today.

Given to a dog, donated
by an old lady,
who––and she always speaks of this––has lived
a proper life for eight-hundred and fifty years.
The neighbors say
she's humane and an animal lover.

Yet I don't want to eat from this plate.
But I must,
Even a dog wants to live.
Times are bad now.
But only a few notice it.––
And I really don't like the mountains either.

Like it makes sense to stick heads
and bones in such high
heights, where it always snows,
even in midsummer.

And then one stands there,
shielded by ice, without life,
a public enemy not even

an einem herumklettern.
Aber unsere Literaturhistoriker sind schließlich
auch so.

Sehr vieles ist so in diesem Land. Oft weiß
ich,
daß wir alle mit Mann und Maus untergegangen
sind.

Die Mädchen gehen in die Uhrenfabrik. Die Bordelle
und die Jesuiten sind verboten.
Am meisten leben in unserem Lande die Toten.

the chamois climb.
After all, our literary chroniclers
are the same way.

So much is like this in our country. Often,
I know
that we've all been extinct,
mice and men.

The girls go to the watch factory. Brothels
and the Jesuits are against the law.
The dead are living the fullest in our country.

SCHWEIZERPSALM III

Einst dürstete ich nach deinem Glauben
    Mein Land
Nun dürste ich nach deiner Gerechtigkeit
    Wahrlich
Die Ärsche deiner Staatsanwälte und Richter
    Lasten so schwer auf ihr
Daß ich das Wort Freiheit kaum mehr ertragen kann
    Das du ständig im Maule führst
Deine Glaubhaftigkeit zu beweisen
    An die niemand mehr glaubt
Nur noch deine Bankgeheimnisse sind glaubhaft.

Was ist aus dir geworden, mein Land?

Wenn du morgens für die Neger in Biafra und
    anderswo Geld sammelst
Legst du dich, Bet- und Bettschwester zugleich,
    Abends mit deren Häuptlingen zwischen die Laken
Deine Waffengeschäfte abschließend
    Damit jene, mit denen du schläfst,
Die abknallen, für die du gesammelt hast,
    Und wenn man deine Zuhälter faßt
Wissen sie von nichts.

Von den Steuerhinterziehern aller Länder unterhalten
    Schenkst du General Westmoreland Whisky ein
Mit ihm nächtlich auf die Rettung des Abendlandes
    anstoßend.

Wehe denen, die anders denken als du
    Deine Lehrstühle
Hältst du von jedem Stäubchen Marxismus rein
    Dein Patriotismus ist so steril und keimfrei
Daß auf seinem Boden wirklich nichts mehr wächst
    Jede neue Idee ist für dich eine Seuche
So lebst du in ewiger Furcht vor Schnupfen und Masern
    Dabei hast du Krebs, du willst es nur nicht wissen,
Und die Psychiater kratzen sich verlegen hinter den Ohren

SWISS PSALM III

I once thirsted after your faith
    My country
Now I thirst after your justice
    Truly
The asses of your attorneys and judges
    Weigh so heavily on her
That I can hardly bear the word "Freedom"
    You constantly carry in your mouth
To prove your trustworthiness
    In which nobody believes anymore
Only your bank secrets are still credible.

What happened to you, my country?

In the mornings when you collect cash
    for the negroes in Biafra and elsewhere
You lie, as a sister in prayer and bed,
    With their chiefs between the sheets at night,
Sealing your weapon deals
    So that those with whom you sleep
Kill those for whom you raised money,
    And when your pimps are caught,
They don't know about anything.

Supported by tax evaders
    Of all countries, you pour
General Westmoreland whiskey
    and toast nightly to the rescue of the West.

Woe to those who think differently
    You keep your universities clean
From every mote of Marxism, your patriotism
    Is so sterile and aseptic that absolutely nothing
Grows in its soil, every new idea is a plague,
    Thus you live in constant fear of the cold and measles
Yet in fact you have cancer but don't
    Want to hear about it, and the psychiatrists,
Embarrassed, scratch their heads and talk about you,

Reden sie von dir, doch du läßt nicht mit dir reden
Wer dir seine Moral predigen will
Den läßt du deine Moral spüren.

Nichts gegen deine Armee. Dieser wackere Verein
Verdrosch einst Österreicher, Burgunder und Deutsche
Verdrosch die Unterdrückten fremder Unterdrücker
Doch vor allem verdrosch er sich selber
Bis er von Napoleon gottseidank so gründlich verdroschen wurde
Daß er seitdem friedlich wurde
Unsere Grenzen mit seinen Waffen beschützend
Wie er sich einbildet
Denn in Wahrheit wurden wir hauptsächlich
Durch unsere Geschäfte beschützt.

Nichts gegen diesen Verein. Man tritt
Ihm unfreiwillig bei, steht in den Statuten
Doch, wenn er sich an jenen vergreift
Die diese nicht mehr unbedingt notwendig finden
Greife ich ihn an
Im Namen der Freiheit
Die er zu verteidigen vorgibt.
Er ist nicht die Stütze meines Landes.
Die Stütze meines Landes sind die, welche denken
Nicht jene, die mitmarschieren.

Armer Villard
Das Töten verurteilend
Wirst du von einem Lande verurteilt
Das aus dem Töten Profit zieht.
Deine Lauterkeit sei unser Vorbild.
Deine Tapferkeit werde die unsrige.
Die Tapferkeit, in einem Lande zu leben
In welchem es langsam genierlich wird
Einem Bundesrat die Hand zu reichen.
Noch sind Wenige, die denken, doch die Mehrheit
Stampft sie in den Untergrund
Stempelt sie zu Kanalisationsschweizern. So
Untergraben sie denn als Maulwürfe
Den Boden, der dich trägt, mein Land
Verändernd mit der Zeit
Was du unveränderlich hältst

But you don't listen
To whomever is preaching his morality
You'll make your morality felt.

Nothing against your army. This brave club
Once thrashed Austrians, Burgunds and Germans
Thrashed the oppressed of foreign oppressors
But they thrashed themselves, especially
Until, thank God, Napoleon gave them such a thorough
Beating, they since turned peaceful
Protecting our borders with their weapons
How conceited
When in truth we were protected
By our business affairs.

Nothing against this club. One joins
Involuntarily, state the bylaws
But when it assaults those
Who find them no longer necessary
I attack it
In the name of freedom
It pretends to defend.
It doesn't support my country.
The support of my country are those who think
Not those who march along.

Poor Villard
Condemning murder, you are
Condemned by a country
That profits from murder.
Your integrity shall be our example.
Your courage will be ours.
The courage to live in a country
Where it becomes embarrassing
To shake a federal councilor's hand.
There're only a few who think, but the majority
Stomps them into the underground
And labels them "Sewage-Swiss." So
As moles they undermine the ground
That carries you, my country
Over time changing
What you believe unchangeable

Einen besudelten Schweizerpaß in der Tasche.

A soiled Swiss passport in their pockets.

WER DIE ERDE WOHNBAR MACHEN WILL

Wer die Erde wohnbar
  machen will
Und freundlicher

Den lacht man aus

Jagt ihn fort
  in stinkende Sümpfe

Dann vergißt man ihn

Doch sein Werk ist nicht
  verloren

Den fernen Nachfahren
  bringen es
Leichtfertige Komödianten
  wieder zurück.

WHO WANTS TO MAKE
THE WORLD A PLACE TO STAY

Who wants to make
    the world a place to stay
And kinder

Is sent up

Driven away
    into stinking swamps

Then he's forgotten

But his work is not
    lost

Slack-off comedians
    will return it
To descendants
    in the distance.

WIE HELDEN VON SHAKESPEARE

Gedichte und Songs aus der Oper einer Privatbank
FRANK DER FÜNFTE

Wie Helden von Shakespeare

Leider habt ihr stets vernommen
Daß die Welt nicht dem Wunsch der Frommen
Daß die Reichen reich und die Armen arm
Und Gott erbarm
In Bälde sich unserer Kälte.

Doch nun laßt den romantischen Quark
Der Mensch ist nicht frei, er lebt im Geschäft
Von Wölfen umstellt, von Hunden umkläfft
Im Kollektiv gefangen
Vom Nächsten beschattet, den er selber bewacht

Mit allen gehangen
Wird er über Nacht
Um seine Menschlichkeit gebracht.

Seid daher stark
Seht teils als Tragödie, teils als Schwank
Die Komödie einer Privatbank
Die Geschichte des Fünften Frank
Personen: Die ganze Bande
Vom Stift bis zum Prokurist
Ja, selbst den Direktor und dessen Frau
Seht ihr leiden in dieser Schau
Sowie einige Kunden, doch die nur am Rande.

Der Grund?
Kommt man euch mit Bettlern, heult jeder Hund
Nur vor unsresgleichen seid ihr objektiv
Mitleid verzerrt und Tränendunst
Armut macht schief
Erst von einer Million aufwärts gibt es klassische Kunst.

LIKE SHAKESPEARE'S HEROES

Poems and songs from Opera About a Private Bank
FRANK THE FIFTH

Like Shakespeare's Heroes

Sadly, you've always heard
That the pious did not wish this world
That the rich are rich and the poor, poor
And that God quickly pitied
Himself of our cold.

But cut this romantic rubbish already
Man is not free, business is his life
Surrounded by wolfs, yelping dogs
Trapped in the collective
Shadowed by his neighbor, whom he already watches

Hung with all of them
He's robbed overnight
Of his humanity.

So be strong
Watch, part tragedy, part farce
This comedy of a private bank
The story of Frank the Fifth
Characters: the entire gang
From apprentice to lawyer
Yes, even the manager and his wife
You'll see suffer in this show
As well as a few customers, but only occasionally.

The reason?
If one gives you beggars, you dogs start howling
Only with people like us do you stay objective
Teary-eyed compassion distorts
Poverty skews things
Classic art starts at a million bucks.

Erfahre denn, o Christenheit
Was wir hoffen und lieben
Vernimm, wie wir morden, schau, wie wir schieben
Und zieh den Hut ab, wenn wir fallen
Ehre sei uns allen.

Nicht nur Könige haben's arg getrieben
Nicht nur Minister, nicht nur Generale
Wateten durch Blut, stanken Skandale
Ich bin der Personalchef, ich muß es ja wissen

Es saust mit uns die Welt des Schwindelns und der Wucherzinsen
Unaufhaltsam in die Binsen
Wir sind die letzten Schurken weit und breit
Nach uns nur böse, öde Ehrlichkeit.

Drum
O Publikum
Freu dich noch ob uns auf Erden
Was jetzt nur schändlich ist, wird unerträglich werden.

Wag dich selbst zu sehn in unserem Handeln
Die wir wie du hienieden wandeln
Verstrickt in Börsenstrategie
Angepöbelt wie noch nie
Von jedem sozialen Wicht
Stehn wir fürchterlich vor dir
Henker zwar, doch Götter schier
Minder groß und blutig nicht
Als die Helden von Shakespeare.

Wir sausen zu den Ahnen

O Mensch, der du gekrochen
Nach Monden und nach Wochen
Aus deiner Mutter Bauch
Was suchst du, Narr, hienieden
Gerechtigkeit und Frieden
Verlache all dein Planen
Du sausest zu den Ahnen

Experience, then, o Christendom
What we love and hope for
Listen how we murder, look how we scam
And take off your hats, when we fall
Honor belongs to us all.

Not only kings have lived it up
Not only ministers, not only generals
Waded through blood, fetid scandals
I'm the personnel manager, I should know

The world of lies and excessive interest rates
Rushes with us inexorably down the drain
We are the last rogues anywhere
After us nothing but evil, dreary honesty.

So
O audience
Be happy about us on earth
What's only disgusting now will soon become unbearable.

Dare to see yourselves in our trade
As us, down here, moving about
Entangled in market strategies
Abused like never before
By every social sucker
Terrifying we stand before you
Hangmen indeed but gods almost
Less great and not bloody
As Shakespeare's heroes.

We Rush to Our Ancestors

O man, you who crawled
After moons and weeks
Out of your mother's belly
What are you looking for down here, fool
Justice and peace
Laugh away your plans
You rush to your ancestors

Und deine Kinder sausen auch.

Den wir hier fromm versenken
Der lenkte unser Denken
Als Präsident und Boss
Geehrt von allen Banken
Stand er, wenn andre sanken
Dann ging's ihm wie uns allen
Er fiel, der nie gefallen
Der Mensch ist klein, der Tod ist groß.

Was wir schieben und erraffen

So sinken Dynastien,
Verstummen, die da schrien
So narrte sie das Licht.
O Fünfter Frank, wie mächtig
War dein Geschlecht, wie prächtig
Du letzter all der Großen
Bis nun ins Grab gestoßen
Und eine Rückkehr gibt es nicht.

Halunken mit Stil sind rar

Die Zeit, die war einst ideal
Voll Dieb' und Schieber überall
Den Kreuger gab's, den Zar
Und mächtig war, was böse war.
Doch nun verwesen
Die einst gewesen
Und Halunken mit Stil
Und Halunken mit Stil sind rar.

Was ich auch tu, es ist verquer
Das Böse schafft sich riesenschwer
Und kleiner wird die Schar
Der treuen Schurken Jahr für Jahr.
Ach, mitgegangen

And your kids rush too.

Whom we drown quietly here
Led our thoughts
As president and boss
Honored by all banks
He stood when others drowned
Then, like all of us
He who never fell, fell
Man is small, death is large.

What We Scam and Reap

This is how dynasties drown,
How those who screamed become silent
This is how the light fooled them.
O, Frank the Fifth, how powerful
Was your race, how glorious
You, last of the greats,
Pushed now into the grave
Where there's no return.

Villains with Style Are Rare

Time was once ideal
Full of thieves and pushers
There was Kreuger, the Czar
And what was evil was powerful.
Yet now rot
Those who once were
And villains with style
And villains with style are rare.

No matter what I do, it's weird
Evil grows with giant strides
And the band of faithful rogues
Gets smaller, year after year.
Alas, to follow them

Ist mitgehangen
Und Halunken mit Stil
Und Halunken mit Stil sind rar.

Was ich auch späh, was ich auch such
Ich find ihn nicht, es ist ein Fluch
Den Nachwuchs ganz und gar
Ein halber Schelm im Vierteljahr
Ist als Ergebnis
Rein ein Begräbnis
Denn Halunken mit Stil
Denn Halunken mit Stil sind rar.

Ihr Fleisch und Blut

Frank der Erste, Ahn, entstiegen bleich
Aus der Armut namenlosem Reich
Siehst entstellt mich, qualvoll alt und weich
Dir entstammt, doch dir in nichts mehr gleich.

Wurdest reich im Sklavenhandel
Deine Flotte stach in See
Blutrot war dein Lebenswandel
Deine Huren weiß wie Schnee.
Hast die Kunden wund geschunden
Nimmer wandte sich dein Glück
Ach, die Zeit ist nun verschwunden
Kehrt, o kehrt nicht mehr zurück.

Hättest, Frank der Zweite, du die Bank
Deines besten Freundes, als er krank
Ausgeplündert, ahntest du, daß dank
Meiner Schulden ich in Armut sank?

Selbst den Papst hast du bestochen
Und der Adel kam zu dir
Oder von dir in die Wochen
Kriege dienten deiner Gier.
Über Leichen gingst gelassen
Völker darbten für dein Glück

Is to hang with them
And villains with style
And villains with style are rare.

Whatever I scout, whatever I seek
I can't find it, it's a curse
The new blood, bones and all
Rascals handling this quarter
Turn the results into
Pure funerals
For villains with style
For villains with style are rare.

Their Flesh and Blood

Frank the First, ancestor, you, pale, who rose
From the poverty of a nameless kingdom
See me disfigured, your descendant, agonizingly old
And soft, who no longer resembles you in any way.

You grew rich dealing slaves
Your fleet put to sea
Blood-red was your way of life
White as snow were your whores.
You oppressed your customers
Your luck never changed
Alas, that time has vanished now
O don't, don't you return.

Had you, Frank the Second, ransacked
Your best friend's bank when he was sick
Would you've suspected that, thanks to
My debts, I was drowning in my poverty?

You greased even the Pope
And the aristocracy came running
Or running away, for weeks
Wars served your greed.
You walked calmly over corpses
Nations starved for your luck

Deine Zeit hat mich verlassen
Kehrt, o kehrt nicht mehr zurück.

Frank der Dritte, als Genie allein
Gründer vom Hongkonger Bankverein
Warst als Chinaboss so hart wie Stein
Gingst als Held in die Geschichte ein.

Rauschgift war dein Haupteinkommen
Weltenweit dein böser Trust
Milliarden eingenommen
Hast du mit dem Preis der Lust.
Saß noch selbst auf deinen Knien
Sangest du von deinem Glück
Ach, die Zeit muß weiterfliehen
Kehrt, o kehrt nicht mehr zurück.

Schaust du, Frank der Vierte, nieder jetzt
Siehst du deinen Sohn von Reu zerfetzt
Menschlichkeit hat ihn so schwer verletzt
Daß nun Trän auf Trän die Wange netzt.

Stürztest Dupont im November
Kamst in Essen an die Macht
Schobst in Erdöl im Dezember
Und im Jänner schon mit Schacht.
Was du triebst, das triebst du munter
Wer sich wehrte, brach in Stück
Ach, auch deine Zeit ging unter
Kehrt, o kehrt nicht mehr zurück.

Wie die Lage steht, in der wir liegen

Wie die Lage steht, in der wir liegen
Oh, ich kenn sie, immer ist sie schief
Was wir auch brechen oder was wir biegen
Es läuft stets so, wie's lief
Im Geschäft sinkt man halt tief.

Was ich geleistet, mußte so geschehen

Your time is no longer mine
O don't, don't you return.

Frank the Third, a single genius
Founder of the Hong Kong Bank Association
You were hard as a rock, China Boss
A hero you went down in history.

Your chief income was drugs
Worldwide your evil cartel
Raked in billions
With the price of lust.
I myself sat on your knees
When you sang of your luck
Alas, time must move on
O don't, don't you return.

If you're looking down, Frank the Fourth
Now you'll see your son torn by sorrow
So badly has humanity wounded him
That tear after tear wets his cheek.

You toppled Dupont in November
Took over in Essen
Dealt crude oil in December
And in January already mine shafts.
What you did, you did gladly
Who defended themselves, fell to pieces
Alas, your time foundered
O don't, don't you return.

How the Situation Stands in Which We Are

How the situation stands in which we are
Oh, I know it, it's always crooked
Whatever we break or bend
It always runs as it always has
One sure sinks deep as a businessman.

My accomplishments had to be this way

Es war nicht gut
Doch den Kindern soll es besser gehen
Doch den Kindern soll es besser gehen
Denn sie sind mein Fleisch und Blut.

Was ich Böses tat auf dieser Erden
Das geschah nur, weil mein Schoß gebar
Denn alle Kinder wollen glücklich werden
Doch diesmal wird es wahr
Und es wird, was niemals war.

Was ich geleistet, wird vergessen werden
Es war nicht gut
Doch den Kindern soll es besser gehen
Doch den Kindern soll es besser gehen
Denn sie sind mein Fleisch und Blut.

Die Abdankung

Und dann, ihr lieben Leut
Ist's wieder Henkerszeit.
Für alle, die wie wir in Machtsystemen nisten
Und sich mit Mörderlogik selber überlisten
Sei's hier, sei's dort, sei's anderswo
Setzt Namen, Daten, Länder nach Belieben ein
Es stimmt ja leider sowieso.
Ihr werdet alle schrein wie wir das bange Lied
All derer, die mächtig, satt und müd:

Die Freiheit ist schön, ach, das wissen wir alle
Doch willst du sie greifen, vergeht sie im Nu
Denn wer am Speck sitzt, sitzt in der Falle
Und willst du hinaus, klappt die Falle zu.

They were not good
But my kids shall have it better
But my kids shall have it better
For they are my flesh and blood.

The evil I've done on this earth
Happened only because of what came from me
For all children want to be happy
And this time it will come true
True, what never has been.

My accomplishments will be forgotten
They were not good
But my kids shall have it better
But my kids shall have it better
For they are my flesh and blood.

The Resignation

And then, you dear people
It's hang time again.
For all, who like us, nest in this system of power
And outwit themselves with their killer logic
Here, there, anywhere
Set names, dates, countries, at leisure
It's true any way you look at it.
Like us, you'll all shout the fearful song
Of the mighty, stuffed, and weary:

Freedom is beautiful, oh, we all know
But if you try to grab it, it disappears instantly
For who sits near the bacon, sits near a snare
And if you try to get away, it traps you.

ICH HABE AUSGEZEICHNET GEGESSEN

»Freß-Arie« des Johann Bockelson von Leyden aus dem Drama ES STEHT GESCHRIEBEN

Ich habe ausgezeichnet gegessen.
Zwar war es ein bescheidenes Mahl, wie es angemessen
ist in schwerer Zeit,
doch wurde ich satt mit Gottes Hilfe, und ein wohliges
Gefühl breitet sich über meine Glieder.
Ich denke mit innerstem Behagen an die Muränensuppe
zurück,
mit den Einsiedlerkrebsen und frischen Meerschnecken,
die mir zu Beginn serviert wurde.
Siehe, es war köstlich!
Auch liegt mir noch der Riesenhecht zärtlich im Sinn,
wie eine ferne Geliebte, in rotem Landwein gekocht
und mit Forelle gefüllt, Röteln, Blaufelchen und sauren
Oliven, Essigreizkern, Perlzwiebeln und Gurken.
Dies alles schmeichelte meinem Magen wie eine
Frauenhand.
Wie brünstig war ich nach Froschschenkeln, Walliser
Blindschleichen und Burgunderschnecken mit leichtgekochten
Schwalbeneiern,
die meiner königlichen Majestät auf silbernem Teller
gereicht worden waren.
Gepriesen sei die Güte des Herrn, der solche Wunderwerke
dem dunklen Schoß der Natur entlockt!
Er ließ die köstlichen Reben wachsen, deren Wein ich
genoß. Geprießen seien Nacktarsch und Liebfrauenmilch.
Gepriesen sei auch der Schweinebauch in Gelee und
Kaviar, Austern mit Champagner, am Spieß gebratenes
Osterlamm, gefüllt mit kleinen Strassburgerwürstchen,
gebackenen Lerchen und dem Bries vorzeitig
geborener Kälber, samt dem schweren Burgunderwein,
der herrliche Fasan, von Krammetsvögeln umgeben,
Rapunzel und Rosenkohl, der göttliche Pommard, die
Biersuppe mit Leberklößen und das Glas Wasser, welches
ich dazu getrunken,
die Schokoladencreme, die niedersächsische Blutwurst,

I HAVE EATEN AN EXCELLENT MEAL

Johann Bockelson von Leyden's "Feast-Aria," from the play
IT IS WRITTEN

I have eaten an excellent meal.
Though it was a modest one, fitting
for tough times,
I got full with God's help, and a warm
feeling is spreading through my body.
With the most heartfelt pleasure I think
back to the eel soup
with hermit crabs and fresh conches
that were served as appetizers.
Look, it was delicious!
The giant luce still caresses my thoughts
like a distant lover, cooked in red wine and filled
with lake trout, vendace, Blaufelchen and sour olives,
pickled mushrooms, pearl onions and gherkins.
All this pleased my stomach like a woman's
hand.
How hot I was for frog legs, blindworms
from Valais and escargot with soft boiled
swallow's eggs
that were served to my royal majesty
on silver plates.
Praised be the kindness of the Lord who draws
such miracles from nature's dark womb!
He let the grapes grow, whose wine I
enjoyed. Praised be Nacktarsch and Liebfrauenmilch.
Praised be also jellied pork belly and
caviar, oysters with champagne, skewered
Easter lamb filled with small Strasbourg sausages,
baked skylarks and the thymus of premature
calves, along with heavy burgundy,
the glorious pheasant surrounded by fieldfares,
corn salad and Brussels sprouts, the divine
Pommard, the beer soup with liver dumplings
and the glass of water I drank,
the chocolate cream, blood sausage from Lower

der Kartoffelsalat und die weißen Bohnen mit
Speck, der saure Most und die Pastete von Champignons,
Trüffeln, Morcheln, Kaiserpilz, der Reis, die
Madeirasauce mit Kapern, der Zizerser in kostbarem
Kristall!
Gesegnet und gebenedeit sei, was ich eben genossen!
O Russischer Salat mit Thunfisch!
O Steinhäger, o Sauerkraut!
O junger Kopfsalat mit gekochten Zwiebeln!
O Glas Stutenmilch mit Schwarzbrot!
Soll ich euer nicht gedenken, wie man zärtlicher Stunden
gedenkt?
Soll ich den Chambertin mißachten und den Gemsrükken,
den gespickten Hasen, die Rehkeule?
Liebte mein Gaumen sie nicht?
Du Bärentatze, köstlich gewurmt, ihr grünen Bohnen
mit Wodka, ihr sauren Zwetschgen mit Spargelspitzen,
du Haferbrei mit Lindenblütentee, du Emmentaler, o
Lambrusco und rote Kirschen in Rum, ich preise euch!
Ihr tatet mir wohl, ihr tatet einem König wohl, ich
preise euch!
Ihr syrischen Heuschrecken mit wildem sibirischem
Honig, euch gilt mein Gruß, mein begeisterter Gruß!
Ich genoß euer Johannes zu Ehren, meinem erlauchten
Vorgänger Johannes dem Täufer zu Ehren!
Liegt mir nicht der Geschmack der Erdbeeren wie
Frauenkuß auf den Lippen?
Rot waren sie und reif, in Quittenmark mit Schlagsahne,
Kirsch dazu, Marc und Pflümliwasser. O Tränen
der Freude!
Laßt mich weinen im Andenken der Coupe Christiane
mit Cherry-Brandy!
Laßt mich weinen, es sind königliche Tränen, welche
auf diesen Teppich aus Belutschistan rollen.
Nun aber,
gnädig gestimmt durch solche Mahlzeit,
da ich auch einige Maß Bier zum Nachtisch geleert,
deren letztes ich eben beende,
will ich mich daran machen, meine Weiber zu empfangen,
denn ich liebe es, allein zu speisen,
höchstens, daß ich Stallknechte holen lasse, die mich,

Saxony, the potato salad and the white beans
with bacon, the cider and champignon pie,
truffles, morels, the Caesar mushroom, rice,
Madeira sauce with capers, the Zizerser in precious
crystal!
Blessed and consecrated be what I've just savored!
O Russian salad with tuna!
O Steinhäger, o sauerkraut!
O young lettuce with boiled onions!
O glass of mare's milk with black bread!
Shall I not think of you, like hours
of lovemaking?
Shall I disregard the Chambertin and the chamois
back, the larded rabbit, the haunch of venison?
Didn't my palate love them?
You bear paw, deliciously nettled, you green beans
with vodka, you sour plums with asparagus tips,
you porridge with linden blossom tea, you Swiss cheese,
o Lambrusco and red cherries in rum, I praise you!
You were good to me, you were good to the king, I
praise you!
You Syrian locusts with wild Siberian honey, yours
is my salute, my spirited salute!
I enjoyed them in honor of your John, in honor
of my noble predecessor, Saint John the Baptist!
Isn't the taste of strawberries on my lips the same
as a woman's kiss?
They were red and ripe, in quince puree with whipped
cream, with kirsch, marc and plum brandy. O tears
of joy!
Let me weep in memory of the Coupe Christiane
with Cherry Brandy!
Let me cry these regal tears rolling
onto this Belutschistani rug.
But now,
feeling merciful after such a feast,
finishing the last of many beers
for dessert,
I want to receive my women,
for I love to eat alone,
or, at the most, call for the grooms and their jokes

von der Ecke des Saales aus, mit ihren Witzen unterhalten.

to entertain me from the corner of this hall.

O WELT DER MÄNNER UND DER MORDE

Chor der Unsterblichen aus der Komödie DIE FRIST

O Welt der Männer und der Morde,
Voll Schmach, voll Haß, voll grauser Tat,
Hinunter schlingt jetzt deine Horde
Der Hölle Maul samt deiner Saat.
Was du seit Anbeginn verbrochen,
Endgültig ist es heut vorbei,
Die Frist ist um der letzten Wochen.
Vorbei die große Hurerei,
Die du noch plantest, dich zu retten.
Es rettet dich nun keiner mehr.
Gewaltiger Koloß in Ketten,
Der Himmel über dir wird leer.
Entmannt starrst du in seine Räume.
Hoch über dir ein Geier kreist.
Noch irres Lachen, irre Träume,
Dann spürst du, wie er dich zerreißt.
Noch betest du, glaubst, daß er höre
Das, was du schreist, der graue Gott.
Als ob dein Sterben ihn gar störe.
Du Narr, wer stirbt, ist für ihn tot.
Und mit dir muß auch er jetzt fallen,
Der böse, sture, geile Greis,
Sich Vater prahlend von uns allen,
Verschmiert mit Blut und kalt wie Eis.
Es stürzt hin seine Frevelgröße.
Wir wenden uns ab, ungerührt,
Versiegeln schweigend unsre Schöße,
Weil Zeugung stets zum Tod verführt,
Weil stets wir kreißten, was zu Aas
Sich wandelte nach Mond und Jahren.
Wie schändlich, Weiber, war doch das,
Was uns vom Manne widerfahren.
Wir waren Opfer seiner Gier.
Er ging mit uns um nach Belieben,
Wir waren für ihn nur ein Tier.
Weh uns, daß wir nicht abgetrieben.
Nun schlug die Stunde des Gerichts.

O WORLD OF MEN AND MURDERS

Choir of the Immortals from the comedy THE DEADLINE

O world of men and murders,
Shameful, hateful, full of grisly deeds,
Hell consumes your hordes
Along with your seed.
The crimes you've committed from the start
Are finally over today,
Your last weeks' lease is up.
The great whoring
You planned for your rescue.
Nobody can save you now.
Violent colossus in chains,
The sky above you is clearing.
Unmanned, you stare into his empty rooms
A vulture circles high above you.
Still your mad laugh, your crazy dreams,
Then you feel how he picks you apart.
You hope he hears your prayers,
Your screams, this gray god.
As if your death would bother him.
You fool, the dying are dead to him.
And now he must fall with you
This bone-headed, horny, evil old fart,
Boasting of being our father,
Covered in blood and cold as ice.
His sacrilegious splendor collapses.
We turn away, unmoved,
Silently sealing our wombs,
For procreation always seduces death,
For we always circled the carrion
That turned towards the moon and time.
How foul it was, women, this act
Of man that befell us.
We were the victims of his lust.
He did with us whatever he wanted,
We were just another animal to him.
Woe to us who didn't abort.
The hour of judgment has arrived.

Urenkel starb, und Gott verreckte.
Das Endliche, es wurde Nichts.
Erreicht ist, was da war bezweckte.
Jetzt sinkt zurück ins weiße All,
Was Männer schufen, Männer dachten,
Ein unfruchtbarer Erdenball
Erlöst von Spermen und vom Schlachten,
Unsterblich wie wir selber sind,
Noch ewiger als Sternenwind.
Was nicht mehr ist, war nur Ereignis,
Was nicht mehr wird, allein ein Gleichnis,
Das Weibliche, es hat zum Ziele
Die Ewigkeit und das Sterile.

The great-grandson died, and God croaked.
The finite turned to nothing.
We've reached what we've aimed for.
Now sink back into the white universe,
What men created, what men thought,
A fruitless ball of dirt saved
From sperm and slaughter,
Immortal like ourselves, more perpetual
Than wind from stars.
What no longer is was but an incident,
What begets no more but a parable,
The feminine, setting its sights
On the infinite and sterile.

MIDAS

I

Ich hätte den bösen Wald nie betreten dürfen

Ich ging ihm entlang

einem großen weißen Gehöft zu

Ohne Ahnung

Manchmal spähte ich in ihn hinein

Ein Dickicht gestürzter Stämme und Äste

Da verlockte mich ein Weg, der in den Wald
hineinführte

Einige Schritte und ich erkannte die Falle

Der Weg [verlor] sich

Planlos ging ich weiter

Tiefer in den Wald hinein

In eine tote Kathedrale

Irgendwo und überall zwitscherten unsichtbare
Vögel

ich watete durch das tote Holz, das von der
Decke der Kathedrale gerieselt war

Endlich fand ich einen zweiten Weg

Schnurgerade lief er durch die Säulen
der Stämme

MIDAS

I

I should never have entered the evil forest

I followed it

heading for a great white farmstead

Without knowing

Sometimes I peeked into it

A thicket of fallen timbers and branches

There a path lured me
into the forest

A few steps and I spotted the trap

The path [lost] itself

Aimlessly, I continued

Deeper into the forest

Into a dead cathedral

Chirping somewhere, everywhere were unseen
birds

I waded through dead wood that had
sifted down from the cathedral's ceiling

At last I found a second path

It ran pointblank
through the wooden columns

Wie ein Befehl, daß ich ihm folgen müsse

Ich ging ihm nach

Einer Gefahr entgegen

Ich spürte unter meinen Füßen eine neue
Materie

ich trat sie vor mich hin

Tannzapfen

Auf einmal nahm ich sie wahr

Dann erst verwandelte ich mich in Midas

Mich mit dem Wald identifizierend

II

Seine Füße traten wie die meinen die Tannzapfen
vor sich hin

Achtlos

Und plötzlich sah er einen Tannzapfen vor
sich liegen

Aus Gold

Er starrte ihn an, dann lachte er. Er

durchschaute die Täuschung

Die Sonne, herunterbrechend, hatte die
Tannzapfen in Gold verwandelt

Es war als ob er über einen dicken goldenen Teppich
goldener Tannzapfen gewandelt wäre

Belustigt nahm er einen Tannzapfen auf

I pursued it like a command

I had to obey

Heading for danger

I felt a new matter beneath
my feet

I kicked it ahead of me

Pinecones

Suddenly, I noticed them

Only then did I change into Midas

Identifying myself with the forest

II

His feet, like mine, kicked
the pinecones ahead of him

Careless

And at once he saw a pinecone
in front of him

Made of gold

He stared at it, and laughed. He

saw through the deception

The beating sun had changed
the pinecones to gold

It was as if he'd strolled across
a thick golden carpet of golden pinecones

Amused, he picked one up

Aufgeweicht vom Schnee, der nun nach den
ersten Frühlingstagen geschmolzen war,
lag er leicht in seiner Hand, schmiegsam und gelb

Da wurde er plötzlich schwer und seine Schuppen
fühlbar

Er wurde zu Gold

Erschrocken ließ er ihn fallen

Zu Gold geworden blieb er Gold zu seinen
Füßen

Er hob einen zweiten auf

Auch er wurde zu Gold in seiner Hand

Einen dritten Tannzapfen

Wieder geschah die Verwandlung

III

Auf die Tannzapfen starrend während ich
weiterschritt

Auf diese blaßbraunen, manchmal blaßgelben
Gebilde, weich und manchmal rollend unter
meinen Füßen

Wurde mir sein Schicksal deutlich

Alle die endlosen Stunden die ich mir
abgequält hatte

ihn zu beschreiben

Dieser endlose Irrgarten der Phantasie
wurde transparent

Sodden from snowmelt
of the first few days of spring,
the core lay softly in his hand, pliant and yellow

But suddenly it became heavy and its leaves
tangible

It turned to gold

Frightened, he dropped it

Turned to gold it remained golden
at his feet

He picked up a second one

It too changed to gold in his hands

A third pinecone

Again the transformation

III

Staring at the pinecones while I
walked on

Over those pale-brown, pale-yellow at times,
shapes, sometimes soft and rolling under
my feet

His fate became clear to me

All those endless hours
I labored

to describe him

Fantasy's endless maze
became transparent

wurde schreibbar

IV

Ich sah ihn durch den Wald zurückrennen

Dann dem Waldrand entlang

Der Stadt entgegen

Unter einem weißen unentschiedenen Himmel

Glücklich und entsetzt zugleich

glücklich, reich geworden zu sein

Entsetzt, weil er noch nicht ahnte, was
ich schon wußte

und doch fühlte, daß etwas Ungeheures
auf ihn lauerte

Sein Untergang

Den er nicht zu benennen wußte

V

Den Weg verfolgend

durch den bösen Wald

stur, willenlos

fielen die Bilder über mich her

ließ mich Midas nicht mehr los

Ich sah einen Juwelier

became writeable

IV

I saw him running back through the forest

Then following its edge

Heading for the city

Below a white, undecided sky

At once happy and horrified

happy to have become rich

Horrified because he had yet to realize
what I already knew

and yet he felt that something monstrous
was lurking

His downfall

He was unable to name

V

Following the path

through the evil forest

stubborn, spineless

pictures fell over me

and Midas never let go of me

I went to see a jeweler

Verwundert starrte er auf den
Tannzapfen

Kunstvoll gearbeitet, sagte er

Nach dem Gesetz Leonardo Fibonaccis von
Pisa

Eine Anordnung

die wir auch bei der spiraligen Verteilung
der Blätter um einen wachsenden Stamm

oder bei der Verteilung der Samenkörner in
der Sonnenblume wiederfinden

Reines Gold

aber unzerbrechlich, noch nie

hätte er solches gesehen

Woher er den Tannzapfen habe?

Geerbt, sagte Midas

Der Wert? Der Juwelier lachte

Den müsse er noch berechnen; er solle
morgen wieder kommen

VI

In seinem Zimmer warf er sich aufs Bett

Irgendwo in der Vorstadt

Morgen würde er noch einmal in den Wald
gehen

Und dann in ein Hotel ziehen

Startled, he stared at the
pinecone

Artfully made, he said

After Fibonacci's
law

An order

we can also find in the spiral distribution
of leaves around a growing branch

or in the distribution of seeds
in a sunflower

Pure gold

but unbreakable, never

had he seen anything like it

Where did he get the pinecone?

Inherited, said Midas

Its value? The jeweler laughed

That he still needed to calculate;
why not return the next day

VI

In his room, he threw himself on the bed

Somewhere in the suburb

Tomorrow he would go back
to the forest

And then move into a hotel

Er war reich

Die Geliebte kam

die Gattin eines reichen Politikers

der eben Präsident der außenpolitischen
Kommission geworden war

Er küßte sie

Spürte in seiner Linken ihre warme Brust

Die plötzlich kalt und glatt wurde

Auch die Lippen und Zähne wurden
metallen

Selbst die Zunge

Er fuhr zurück

Ein Kopf aus Gold starrte ihm entgegen

Er riß ihr die Kleider vom Leib

Eine Statue aus Gold

Das schwarze Haar golden

Selbst die Schamhaare kunstvoll gearbeitet

Jemand klopfte an die Tür

Er öffnete

Achtlos in seiner rechten Hand ihr zerrissenes
Kleid

Auf dem Boden ihr Pelzmantel

Der Präsident der außenpolitischen Kommission

He was rich

His lover arrived

wife of a rich politician

who'd just become president
of the Foreign Affairs Commission

He kissed her

His left hand touching her warm breast

That at once felt cold and smooth

Lips and teeth, too, turned
metallic

Even her tongue

He backed up

A head of gold stared at him

He ripped off her clothes

A golden statue

The black hair golden

Even the pubic hair artfully sculpted

Somebody knocked on the door

He opened

Holding carelessly her tattered dress in his
right hand

Her fur coat on the floor

The president of the Foreign Affairs Commission

stürzte zum Bett

Wo ist meine Frau?

Packte die schwere Statue

Stemmte sie an die Wand

Durchwühlte das Bett, stellte es auf,
nahm es auseinander

Durchwühlte den Schrank, kippte ihn um,
stürzte zum Fenster, vielleicht war sie
auf dem Dach, schaute sich um, starrte
hinab

Raste die Treppe hinunter. Fünf Stockwerke

Wo ist meine Frau?

Suchte den Gehsteig ab

Keuchte wieder herauf

Schob die Statue weg

Schwer fiel sie auf den Boden

Er erkannte nicht seine Frau

Er hielt sie für eine Statue aus Messing

VII

Polizeiwagen mit Blaulichtern auf der
regennassen Straße

Feuerwehrmänner, die über Dächer kletterten

Dunkle Schatten vor einem milchigen

lunged towards the bed

Where's my wife?

He seized the heavy statue

Set it against the wall

Rifled through the bed, stood it up,
took it apart

Rummaged through the wardrobe, knocked it
over, lunged for the window, perhaps she was
on the roof, and looked around, stared
down

Sped down the stairs. Five flights

Where's my wife?

Searched the sidewalk

Climbed back up, gasping

Pushed away the statue

Heavily, it fell to the floor

He didn't recognize his wife

He thought her a brass statue

VII

Police cars with lights on
the rainy street

Firemen who climbed over roofs

Dark shadows against a milky

Nachthimmel

VIII

Nächtliche Verhöre

Wochenlang

Hartes Licht auf ihn gerichtet

Hin und wieder eine Zigarette

Eine Tasse Kaffee

Der Juwelier hatte den goldenen Tannzapfen abgeliefert

Zwei weitere hatte man bei ihm gefunden

Woher hast du die? Von wem gestohlen?

Duzen Sie mich nicht

Woher haben Sie die? Von wem gestohlen?

Geerbt

In einer Nacht schrie der Mann auf. Die Statue glich meiner Frau!

Die Statue wurde untersucht

Reines Gold

IX

Nach Monaten war er frei

Er ging zum Juwelier

night sky

VIII

Nightly interrogations

For weeks

Hard light pointing at him

Here and there a cigarette

A cup of coffee

The jeweler had delivered the golden
pinecone

Two more had been found on him

Where'd you get them, buddy? Who'd you steal them from?

Don't buddy me

Where'd you get them? Who'd you steal them from?

Inherited

One night the husband woke up screaming.
The statue resembled my wife!

The statue was examined

Pure gold

IX

Months later he was free

He walked to the jeweler

Der saß in seinem Kabinett hinter dem
Tisch

An der Wand neben dem Juwelier lehnte
die goldene Statue

Seine Geliebte

Auf dem Tisch lagen die drei goldenen
Tannzapfen

Zwar halte er ihn immer noch für einen
Dieb

Sagte der Juwelier

Da sich aber niemand gemeldet habe, sei
er bereit, sich mit ihm zu verständigen

Auch über die goldene Statue könne er mit
ihm einig werden

Er nannte einen schäbigen Preis

Er nahm die Scheine entgegen

Zufrieden? fragte der Juwelier

Er nickte

Nun können Sie mir sagen, wo Sie das Gold
gestohlen haben, grinste der Juwelier

Er betrachtete ihn

Reichen Sie mir die Hand, sagte er

Der Juwelier gab ihm die Hand

Eine goldene Statue saß hinter dem Tisch
des Kabinetts

Who sat at the desk in his
small shop

The golden statue was leaning
against the wall next to him

His beloved

On the desk lay the three golden
pinecones

He still believed him to be
a thief

Said the jeweler

But because nobody came forward
he was ready to make a deal

They could even agree
on the golden statue

He named a sorry price

He took the bills

Happy? asked the jeweler

He nodded

Now you can tell me where you
stole the gold, grinned the jeweler

He looked at him

Give me your hand, he said

The jeweler shook his hand

A golden statue sat at the desk
in the small shop

Er nahm die drei Tannzapfen zu sich

X

Er ging bei einer Baustelle an aufgeschichteten
Ziegelsteinen vorbei

Wie er einen ergriff, wurde dieser zum
Goldbarren

Er legte ihn zu den goldenen Tannzapfen
in seine Aktentasche

XI

Hungrig tauchte er den Löffel in die
Suppe, führte ihn zum Mund

Gold überzog die Zähne, die Zunge, den
Gaumen

Entsetzt erhob er sich, hielt sich die
Serviette vor den Mund

Eilte an den Kellnern vorbei

Löste langsam in der Toilette Blatt um
Blatt das Gold aus seinem Munde

Wickelte es in sein Taschentuch

Bestellte Schnecken, Tiere, vor denen
es ihn immer geekelt hatte

Schluckte sie mühsam hinunter

Durch das Fenster den Wagen nachstarrend,
die aufheulend in die Straße einbogen, wo
der Juwelier wohnte

He took the three pinecones

X

He passed a pile of bricks
at a construction site

As he grabbed one, it changed
into a gold bar

He put it in his briefcase
next to the golden pinecones

XI

He dipped the spoon into the soup
and raised it to his hungry mouth

Gold covered his teeth, his tongue,
his palate

Horrified, he stood up and covered
his mouth with a napkin

Rushed past the waiters

In the bathroom loosened slowly
leaf by leaf the gold from his mouth

Wrapped it in his handkerchief

Ordered escargot, animals
that had always disgusted him

Struggled to swallow them

He watched the howling cars
through the window turn into
the street where the jeweler lived

XII

In einem Hotelzimmer wurde ihm sein
Schicksal deutlich

Wie mir sein Schicksal deutlich wurde

Als ich im bösen Wald über die Tannzapfen
schritt

die dicht den Weg bedeckten

Deren Verwandlung war die Ankündigung

die Verwandlung der Geliebten, des Juweliers
und der Speise das Gesetz

Was er begehren würde

Aus Liebe oder aus Haß

Würde sich in Gold verwandeln

In totes Metall

Der Reichtum würde seine Armut sein

Die Liebe Mord

Essen Verhungern

Trinken Verdursten

Nur ein Ausweg blieb

Das Abstrakte

Die Macht

XII

In a hotel room he realized
his fate

Like I'd realized his fate

Walking on the path covered
densely with pinecones

through the evil forest

Their transformation was a warning

of the lover's transformation, the jeweler's,
and the food, the law

Whatever he would desire

Out of love or hate

Would turn to gold

Into dead metal

Wealth would be his poverty

Love would be his murder

Food, starvation

Drink, death of thirst

Only one way out remained

The abstract

Power

XIII

Er ging wie ein Schachspieler vor

Er überlegte jeden Zug

Er baute sein Imperium mathematisch auf

Er benutzte seine Gabe behutsam

Er vermied, den Goldpreis unnötig zu
senken

Doch über sein Unterbewußtsein hatte er
keine Macht

Zwar trug er immer Handschuhe

Seit einige Unachtsamkeiten vorgekommen
waren

Der Kugelschreiber, womit er spielte,
hatte sich in Gold verwandelt, während
er darüber nachdachte, wie er Nestlé
kaufen könnte

Auch das Telefon, als ihm die Nachricht
durchgegeben wurde, daß der Dollarkurs
aufs neue gesunken war

Die Sekretärin, der er unwillkürlich
einen freundschaftlichen Klaps gab, weil
sie sich vertippt hatte

Und der alte Aufsichtsrat, dem er auf die
Schulter klopfte, ihn über den Verlust
seiner Gattin zu trösten

hatten sich in Goldstatuen verwandelt

Nachdem man sie monatelang gesucht hatte

XIII

He proceeded like a chess player

He thought about every move

He built his empire mathematically

He used his gift carefully

He avoided rigging down the price of gold
unnecessarily

Yet he had no control over his
subconscious

Though he always wore gloves

Since a few careless acts had
occurred

The pen he played with
that had turned to gold
while he thought about
how to buy Nestlé

The phone, too,
as he was told that the dollar
had fallen anew

The secretary, whom he couldn't help
to give a friendly pat
because of a typo

And the old director whom he gave
a slap on the shoulder to comfort him
after the loss of his wife

all changed into gold statues

After they'd searched for them for months

ließ er die beiden in seinem Vorzimmer
auf Sockel stellen

Erklärend

Er wolle ihnen zum Gedenken diese so vollkommen
ähnlichen Kunstwerke stiften

Die Handschuhe mußte er immer wieder wechseln

Allzuleicht verwandelten sie sich in Gold

XIV

Doch wenn er auch im Abstrakten handelte

Von seinem Hochhaus aus

Sein Imperium war nicht abstrakt

Es wuchs und überwucherte die anderen

Es materialisierte sich

Öltanker

Bohrinseln

Raffinerien

Banken

Plantagen

Computer

Flugzeuge

Baumwolle

Chemiekonzerne

he let both of them be set on pedestals
in his waiting room

Explaining

He wanted to honor them by endowing
these perfect works of art

Time and again he had to change his gloves

Too easily did they turn to gold

XIV

But even though he acted in the abstract

Seen from his skyscraper

His empire was not abstract

It expanded and overgrew the others

It materialized

Supertankers

Drilling rigs

Refineries

Banks

Plantations

Computers

Airplanes

Cotton

Science corporations

Waffen

Killersatelliten

XV

Nur das Essen war schwierig

Er mußte immer wieder seinen Mund vom Gold
säubern

Wenn auch der Spezialkoch, den er angestellt
hatte

sich Mühe gab, immer ekelhaftere Speisen
zu bereiten

Die er

Um nicht hungrig zu werden

mehrmals im Tage aß

Aber einmal

nachdem er Kutteln gegessen hatte

Vor denen es ihn immer geekelt hatte

Aber die er

vor lauter Hunger plötzlich gierig verschlang

mußte der Chirurg verwundert einen seltsam
gestalteten Klumpen Gold aus seinem Magen
operieren

Weapons

Killer satellites

XV

Only eating was difficult

Again and again he had to clean his mouth
from all the gold

Even though the private cook
he'd hired

took great pains to prepare
increasingly disgusting meals

Which he ate

To not grow hungry

several times a day

But once

after he'd eaten tripe

Which he'd always found disgusting

But suddenly devoured

out of sheer hunger

a startled surgeon had to remove
a strange clump of gold from his
stomach

XVI

Der böse Wald lichtete sich

Ich trat ins Helle

Nur noch einzelne Stämme ragten in die Höhe

Laubbäume

Der Boden ohne Tannzapfen, aber auch ohne
Laub

Gefällte Stämme aufeinandergeschichtet

Andere schon zersägt

Das weiße Gehöft auf dem Feld hatte ich
hinter mir gelassen

Ich setzte mich auf eine Bank am Rande
der Lichtung

Je mehr er sein Imperium ausdehnte, desto
mehr mußte die Zahl seiner Feinde wachsen

Er mußte allen in die Quere kommen

Den Amerikanern

Den Russen

Den Arabern

Den Israeli

Der EWG

Er mußte in Zugzwang geraten

Je länger ein Schachspiel dauert,
desto unerbittlicher wird es

XVI

The evil forest cleared

I stepped into the light

Only a few single trunks rose into the heights

Broad-leaved trees

The floor without pinecones, but also without
leaves

Layers of fallen timbers, one on top of the other

Some already sawed to pieces

I'd left behind me the white farmstead
on the field

I sat on a bench at the edge
of the clearing

The more he expanded his empire,
the more the number of his enemies grew

He had to get in everyone's way

Americans

Russians

Arabs

Israeli

The EEC

He needed to force himself into a tight spot

The longer a game of chess,
the more relentless it gets

Zu Beginn ist fast jeder Fehler zu verbessern,
gegen das Ende keiner mehr

Die Kausalität ist unerbittlich, die Freiheit
illusorisch

Sein Endspiel war nicht zu gewinnen

Er mußte ein Patt anstreben

XVII

Ich ging wieder in den bösen Wald zurück

Ich durchquerte die Lichtung und tauchte
in ihn

Den schnurgeraden Pfad wiederfindend, den
ich gekommen war

Wieder schritt ich über den weichen
Tannzapfenteppich

XVIII

Arbeiter aus allen Ländern

Die er heimlich über die Grenze hatte
schaffen lassen

Erbauten ein Labyrinth von unterirdischen
Gewölben

Sowie einen riesigen Schmelzofen mit
Fließbändern und Greifzangen

die zu ihm führten

Und eine Gießanlage, auch sie automatisch

Almost every mistake can be corrected
at the beginning, but not at the end

Causality is relentless,
freedom is illusive

His endgame could not lead to victory

He was forced to seek a stalemate

XVII

I again returned to the evil forest

I crossed the clearing and dove right
onto it

The dead straight path
finding the way I'd walked

Again I stepped across the soft
carpet of pinecones

XVIII

Workers from every country

Whom he'd smuggled across
the border

Were building a labyrinth of subterranean
vaults

And a giant furnace
with conveyer belts and tongs

that led to him

And a foundry, mechanized, too

Anlage gebaut war

gab er den Arbeitern ein Fest

Er lud auch die Architekten und Ingenieure dazu ein

Und als sie alle betrunken waren

Zog er die Handschuhe aus und berührte jeden

Die Greifzangen legten die goldenen Statuen aufs Fließband

Im Schmelzofen wurden sie zu flüssigem Gold

Als Goldbarren kamen sie aus der Gießanlage

Sie wurden automatisch aufgestapelt

XIX

Der Weg im bösen Wald führte nirgendwo hin

Es war, als wäre ich in sein Labyrinth geraten

Nach endlosen Zeiten

die so unermeßlich waren

daß selbst das Gold vermodert war

Sah ich ihn in seinem Gewölbe

Allzu viele hatten ihm nachgestellt

When the facility was complete

he threw a party for the workers

And invited the architects
and engineers

When they were all drunk

He removed his gloves and
touched them

The tongs placed the golden statues
onto the belts

In the furnace they changed to liquid
gold

They came out of the foundry as
gold bars

They were stacked mechanically

XIX

The path in the evil forest led
nowhere

It was as if I'd entered his
labyrinth

After incalculable

never-ending times

when even the gold was decayed

I saw him in his vault

Too many had followed him

Allzu viele saßen in den Bäumen und lagen
hinter den Bäumen des Parks, der sein Haus
umgab

Mit Spezialgewehren bewaffnet

Er aber

im innersten Raum seines unterirdischen
Labyrinths

kauerte einem Teppich von goldenen
Tannzapfen gegenüber

Kunstvoll ineinandergeflochten

Die übrigen Wände mit schwarzem
Sammet bezogen

Die Goldbarren verbergend, die sich hinter
ihm stapelten

Auch der Boden war mit schwarzem Sammet
ausgelegt

War er doch ebenfalls golden

Unangreifbar kauerte er inmitten der
Unermeßlichkeit seines Reichtums

Wie dieser steril

Er streifte den rechten Handschuh [ab]

Er hatte nur noch den Wunsch, dem allen ein Ende
zu setzen

Griff sich an den Hals

wurde langsam zu Gold.

Too many sat in the trees
and lay behind the trees of the park
that surrounded his house

Armed with special rifles

He, however,

cowered next to a golden carpet
of pinecones

in the innermost room of his
underground labyrinth

Artfully woven

The rest of the walls were covered in
black samet

To conceal the piles of gold bars
behind it

Even the floor was laid out in black
samet

It was golden as well

Unassailable, he cowered
amid his immense wealth

Sterile like it

He took [off] his right glove

He had only the wish to put an end
to it all

Grabbed his throat

slowly turned to gold.

FÜR WILLY BIRGEL

Viele gingen schon,
    Die mir unersetzbar waren,
Viele der Schauspieler.

Früh Seyferth, der Mönch meines
    Ersten Stücks,
Kalser, unendlich überlegen, liebenswürdig und
    unendlich textunsicher,
Graf, Teege, Domin und viele andere.

Die Carlsen, der ich ihre letzte Rolle,
    Ihr eine Freude zu machen,
Da sie noch einmal spielen wollte,
    Der Achtzigjährigen
Zum Mißvergnügen der Kritik in die *Wiedertäufer*
    Hineinimprovisierte.

    Ginsberg, mein Freund,
Leonhard Steckel endlich,
    Mein Meteor,
Zerschellt im Schnellzug
    Zwischen München und Zürich.

Nun Willy Birgel.

Er war auf der Bühne,
    Er brauchte kein Spiel,
Er war Matthison, gläubig, überzeugt,
    Daß Gott durch ihn ein Wunder schaffe,
Und er war im gleichen Stück
    Der Kardinal, ein Herr, empört darüber,
Daß man von ihm verlangte,
    Informiert zu sein.

Im *Urfaust* darauf spielte er
    Gleich vier Rollen,
Den Erdgeist, Wagner, den versoffensten
    Der Studenten,

FOR WILLY BIRGEL

Many have passed on already
    Whom I can't replace,
Many of the actors.

Seyferth went early, the Monk
    In my first play,
Kalser, infinitely superior, gentle and
    always worried about his lines,
Graf, Teege, Domin and many others.

Carlsen, the eighty-year-old, for whom
    I improvised, to the annoyance
Of the critics, a role in *The Anabaptists*,
    To make her happy,
Because she wanted to act
    One last time.

    My friend Ginsberg,
Leonhard Steckel, finally,
    My meteor,
Burst in an express train
    Between Munich and Zurich.

Now Willy Birgel.

He was on stage,
    He didn't need a script,
He was Matthison, religious, convinced
    That God will use him to create a miracle,
And in the same play
    He was the Cardinal, a lord, disgusted
That one demanded
    He should know everything.

And then in *Urfaust* he played
    Four roles at once,
Erdgeist, Wagner, the most wasted
    Of students,

Mit einem Bauch, rund wie die Erdkugel,
    Den bösen Geist als violetten Bischof.

Zuletzt spielte er im *Mitmacher.*

Das Publikum pfiff, als wir zusammen
    Auf der Bühne standen.
Hinter dem Vorhang lachte er,
    Tränen in den Augen,
Als ahnte er,
    Daß er seine letzte Rolle gespielt hatte.

Ein abtretender Schauspieler,
    Der einen durchgefallenen
Autor umarmt: Bild des Theaters.

Nie ehrte mich eine Freundschaft mehr,
    Wir sahen uns zuletzt in einer Niederlage,
Nicht die Siege zählen.

    Viele gingen schon,
Die mir unersetzbar waren,

    Nun auch er.

    Niemand sage,
Keiner der Schauspieler sei unersetzlich,
    Jeder ist anders,
Mit jedem, der geht,
    Geht eine unserer Möglichkeiten dahin.

Ein jeder dieser großen Komödianten ist nur,
    weil er unauswechselbar ist,
Keine Welle gleicht der anderen.

With a belly round as a globe,
    The evil ghost as a purple Bishop.

At the end he played in *The Collaborator.*

The audience booed while we
    Stood together on stage.
He laughed behind the curtain,
    Tears in his eyes,
As if he knew
    That he'd played his last role.

A retiring actor,
    Who embraces a failed
Playwright: perfect picture of the theatre.

Never did I honor a friendship more,
    In defeat we saw each other last,
Not counting victories.

    Many have passed on already
Whom I can't replace,

    Now even he.

    Nobody shall say,
No actor is irreplaceable,
    Everyone is different,
With each one who passes on,
    Another possibility is gone.

Each of these comic actors
    is great because he's irreplaceable,
No wave resembles another.

DRAMATURGISCHER RAT

Verzapf keinen Tiefsinn
Füge dem Rätsel kein neues bei

Es liegt nicht im Wort
Schaff ein Gebilde

Drei Männer am Tisch
Was sie reden ist unwichtig

Sie wollen richtig handeln
Aber die Würfel sind gefallen

Wer den falschen Zug bestieg
Mag in ihm zurück rennen
Er erreicht doch, wohin er
nicht wollte

DRAMATURGIC ADVICE

Don't give us any profound talk
Don't add to the mystery

It's not the word
Create a shape

Three men at a table
What they say is not important

They want to do right
But the dice are cast

Who boards the wrong train
May run back in it
But arrives where he didn't
    want to go

AN VARLIN

In meinem Arbeitszimmer
    Hängt deine Heilsarmee
Zwei Guitarren, eine Trompete, eine Fahne
    Neun Menschen
Gläubiger als ich

Wenn ich aus meinem Atelier trete
    Grinst mir Freund Loetscher entgegen
Er kennt meine grammatikalischen Fehler

Sitze ich im Wohnzimmer
    Meiner Frau zuhörend
Wie sie auf dem Flügel improvisiert
    Räkeln sich hinter ihr in zwei Sesseln
Zwei Menschen an der Wand
    Ein Mann und eine Frau

Esse ich
    Blicke ich auf die Neapolitanerin
Die nicht mit mir schlafen wollte
    Weil du nicht katholisch bist

Und hinter mir
    Leuchtet in Schwarz eine Vespasienne
Durch den Pariser Nebel
    Non olet

Stehe ich mir gegenüber
    Von Dir gemalt
Trinkt mir ein dicker Leib aus Fett und Wasser
    Freundlich zu
Der einmal in einem Krematorium verdampft

Wir sind blind ohne Deine Gesichte
    Wir allein sind dein Gegenstand
Du weichst nicht ins Gegenstandslose

Du formst unsere Taten, rächst unsere Verbrechen

TO VARLIN

Your Salvation Army
    Hangs in my study
Two guitars, a trumpet, a flag
    Nine people
More religious than I

When I leave my studio
    I meet my friend Loetscher's grin
He knows my grammatical mistakes

When I sit in the living room
    Listening to my wife
Improvising on the grand piano
    Two people on the wall
Loll in two armchairs behind her
    A man and a woman

When I eat
    I look at the Neapolitan woman
Who didn't want to sleep with me
    Because you're not a Catholic

And behind me
    A vespasienne glows
Black through the Parisian fog
    Non olet

When I look at myself
    Painted by you
A big body of fat and water kindly
    Raises his glass to me
Who someday will evaporate in a crematory

We are blind without your faces
    We alone are your subjects
You don't move into the abstract

You shape our deeds, avenge our crimes

Indem Du uns zeichnest
Wie Gott Kain

By drawing us
Like God drew Cain

GEDICHTBAND BEI EINER MITTAGSZIGARRE

Gott schuf die Welt ohne zu denken

Soso lala

Er machte sie aus dem Nichts, mit einer Geschwindigkeit ohne Gleichen

Soso lala

Darum (die Sonne steht immer noch hoch) dichte ich in sechzig Sekunden

Soso lala

eine ganze Welt voll. Zwischen zwei Uhr dreizehn und zwei Uhr vierzehn

Soso lala

Man muß es endlich einmal wagen hinüberzuspringen

bei einer Zigarre zu dichten, die dabei nur ein Weniges verrauchen darf

zu arbeiten, ohne sich zu korrigieren

die Worte einfach hinzusetzen, wie eine Mutter Kinder auf die Welt setzt

ohne sie wieder zurückzunehmen.

Das Zögern einer Sekunde verdirbt ein Gedicht.

Auch ist es nicht erlaubt, Worte zu wählen.

So schreibe ich denn, so springe ich denn

BOOK OF POEMS WHILE SMOKING A LUNCHTIME CIGAR

God created the world without thinking

So-so

He made it out of nothing, with incomparable
speed

So-so

That's why (the sun still stands high) I write poetry
in sixty seconds

So-so

an entire world full. Between two-thirteen and
two-fourteen

So-so

One must finally dare to jump across

to write poetry while smoking a cigar that can
cloud only a few things

to work without revision

simply write down words, like a mother
giving birth to her children

and not putting them back in.

To hesitate for a second ruins the poem.

It's also not allowed to select words.

Thus I write, thus I jump across

an ein anderes Ufer.

Eines Tags (die Sonne stand hoch)

betrachtend die weiße Wäsche, die man hingehängt hatte

und darüber hin die Zweige der Bäume

weiß, grün vor dem blauen Himmel,

Alles vom Winde bewegt, von dem frischen, nördlichen Winde

überfiel mich die Ahnung einer höheren Leichtigkeit.

O Leichtigkeit des Gedankens, der zum Verbrechen wird, wenn man Arbeit an ihn wendet!

Wie der Wind die Zweige bewegt, die grünen die Wäsche, die weiße,

bewegt der Geist das mühsame Durcheinander von Blut und Fleisch meines Leibes,

mich treibend in seinem Spiel.

Du einziges Spiel, das immer noch erlaubt ist:

Gedichte, die in ein, zwei Minuten getan sind

im Traume eines Tags (die Sonne stand hoch)

Blitze, die irdische Finsternis erleuchten.

to another riverbank.

One day (the sun stood high)

looking at the white laundry somebody'd hung

and above it the branches of the trees

white, green against the blue sky,

everything moved by wind, the fresh, Nordic
wind

I was struck by a notion of intense ease.

O ease of thought that turns to crime
when worked on!

The way the wind moves the green branches
the white laundry,

the spirit moves the painful chaos
of my body's blood and flesh,

drifting in its game.

You're the only game that's still allowed:

Poems written in one, two minutes,

in a daydream (the sun stood high)

lightning that illuminates our earthly darkness.

VOR UNS HINTASTEND, LIEBES

Vor uns hintastend, Liebes
Ins immer Dunklere
Fühlen wir in der Kälte unsere Wärme

Versuchen wir hilflos uns Gutes zu tun
Gemeinsam betend
Bevor wir schlafen
Gott zu erreichen

Wie ferne alles.

Blasse Bilder. Doch plötzlich
Überscharf
Die Erinnerung. Deine kühle Hand
In der meinen
Saß ich dir gegenüber.
Sah deinen zuckenden Mund
Wir sagten einander kein Wort
So mächtig war unsere Liebe

Nun ist in unserem Schweigen oft
Traurigkeit
ein Schatten nur der
Freude
Vielleicht verborgen wie Gott

GROPING ALONG, MY DEAR

Groping along, my dear
Into ever-growing darkness
We feel our warmth in the cold

We try helplessly to do each other good
Praying together
Before we sleep
To reach God

How distant it all is.

Faded pictures. But suddenly
Hypersharp
Memory. With your cool hand
In mine
I sat facing you.
Saw your twitching mouth
We didn't say a word
Our love was that powerful

Now much of our silence is
Sadness
only a shadow
Of happiness
Hidden, perhaps, like God

KRONENHALLE

1.
Ich bin an wenigen Orten daheim

Im Haus über dem See

Auf der andern Seite des Monds

Auf der Bühne des Schauspielhauses
Umstellt von Kulissen

Und in der Kronenhalle
In Mutter Zumstegs Reich

Die Leberknödelsuppe dampft
Aldo kommt mit dem Wagen angerollt
Und ich denke über einen Auftritt der Giehse nach

2.
An den Nachmittagen zwischen drei und vier
    Am Tisch
Zwischen den Glasscheiben

Wie hinter Silberstaub schläft die Katze
    Auf der Bank in der Ecke
Kein Gast wagt sie zu stören

Vor blauen Tramwagen manchmal
    Bewegen sich die Vorhänge

Geisterhaft auf die gleiche Scheibe gespiegelt
    Erscheint aber auch
Mein Gesicht und die fernere Theke

Schiebt sich
    Der Hintergrund vor den Vordergrund.

KRONENHALLE

1.
I'm at home in few places

In the house by the lake

On the other side of the moon

On the stage of the theatre
Surrounded by side scenes

And in the Kronenhalle
In Mother Zumsteg's kingdom

The liver-dumpling soup steams
Aldo comes rolling with the car
And I think about one of Giehse's performances

2.
On afternoons between three and four
At the table
Between windowpanes

As if behind silver dust
The cat sleeps on the corner bench
No customer dares to disturb her

Before blue tram wagons, sometimes
The curtains move

Ghostlike reflected onto the same pane
My face appears as well
And the more distant bar

The background
Shifting ahead of the foreground.

WAS SOLL AN DIESEM NACHMITTAGE

Was soll an diesem Nachmittage
So nördlich wolkig eine Frage
Das Leben fließt dir ab. Laß sein
Du gehst auch zu den Mythen ein
Ein ferner Schrei, wo Neger singen
Was du versuchst wird selten dir gelingen
Nur unabsichtlich wächst das Große
Der Zufall mischt, nicht du, die Lose

WHAT'S THE POINT THIS AFTERNOON

What's the point this afternoon
So cloudy, northerly, of a question
Life pours from you. Forget it
You, too, will enter the myths
A distant cry, where Negroes sing
Anything you try seldom succeeds
The Great develops only unintentionally
Chance, not you, shuffles our lots

VATER MEIN, EIN RIESE STEHT IM WALD

Vater mein, ein Riese steht im Wald
Ach mein Kind, im Walde ist's nur kalt
Mutter mein, ein Riese winkt im Wald
Ach mein Kind, will's dir nicht rauben
Bist noch jung und darfst nicht glauben
    An den Wald
        worin die Riesen sind

Riese mein, wie rot sind deine Hände
Ach mein Kind, will dich nun rauben
Und dein Leben muß dran glauben
In dem Wald
In dem Wald
In dem Wald
    worin die Riesen sind

FATHER, MY, THERE'S A GIANT IN THE FOREST

Father, my, there's a giant in the forest
Oh, child, it's but cold in the forest
Mother, my, a giant waves in the forest
Oh, child, don't want to spoil it
You're still young and shouldn't believe
    In the forest
        where giants are

Giant, my, how red your hands are
Oh, child, just want to spoil you
It's your turn to die
In the forest
In the forest
In the forest
    where giants are

MEERE

Ich liebe das Haus zu verlassen

In einen Tag zu gehen, der sich
gegen Abend neigt

Durch Meere roten Laubs zu waten

SEAS

I love to leave the house

Walk into a day
approaching dusk

Wade through oceans of red leaves

SPIELREGELN

Im Unerbittlichen
fordere nicht Unerfüllbares
Halte die Spielregeln ein

Richte nicht die Gerichteten
Du bist einer von ihnen
Misch dich nicht ein, du bist
eingemischt

Sei menschlich, nimm Abstand
Jeden trifft ein eigener Pfeil
Du kannst niemanden schützen

Unrechtes geschieht nicht
aber Furchtbares

Was geschieht, bist du
Es geschieht dir recht

RULES OF THE GAME

In the grimmest of moments
don't ask for the impossible
Play by the rules

Don't judge the judged
You're one of them
Don't interfere, you're
   already part of it

Be human, step back
We all get what we deserve
You can't save anybody

There's no injustice
only the terrible

You're what happens
It serves you right

BLICK DURCHS FENSTER

Erst eine Fläche dunkelgelben Steins
zerrieben zu Sand

Nah, gegenwärtig

Dann ein Band mit Blumen, Büschen,
Sträuchern

Dahinter der See

Ferner Hügel, ferner Berge

Der Himmel endlich

Ein Planet irgendwo

Sterne dann, deren Licht Jahre alt ist

Nur noch Vergangenes

VIEW THROUGH THE WINDOW

First a plane of dark-yellow stone
    grinded into sand

Near, present

Then a line of flowers, bushes,
    shrubs

Behind it, the lake

Farthermore, hills, mountains

The sky, finally

A planet somewhere

Then stars, their light years old

Only the past

ANTARES

Sah dich sinken, sah dich steigen
Roter, rätselhafter Stern
Tief im Süden, tief im Westen
Bliebst du unermeßlich fern

Doch in meinen Träumen nächtlich
Heiße Sehnsucht dich beschwor
Weltengroß aus Sternentiefen
Brach dein Riesenbild hervor

Deiner Urwelt Feuernebel
War mit einem Male nah
Milder, größer als die Sonne
Hingest du gewaltig da

Fülltest nie erahnte Räume
Alles war von dir erhellt
Deiner Jugend Morgenröte
Goß sich über diese Welt

ANTARES

Saw you sinking, saw you rising
Red, mysterious star
Deep in the south, deep in the west
You remained immeasurably far

But nightly in my dreams
Hot desire invoked you
Large as planets from the depths of stars
Your giant image broke through

Your primal world's fiery nebula
Was suddenly near
Milder, larger than the sun
You, massive, hung there

Filled never-thought-of spaces
You illuminated everything
Your youth's aurora
Poured over this world

MOND

Du sinnlos tote Welt aus Stein
Dein Odem bläst mir Kälte ein

Zerfressen steigst du still empor
Beleckt vom Übermaß des Lichts
Und weist des Weltalls Male vor

Verhüllst die Narben des Gesichts
Nimmst wieder ab und wirst zu nichts

MOON

You numb, dead world of stone
Your breath blows me with cold

Eaten up, you climb quietly
Licked with this excess of light
And present the universe's marks

Cover the pocks on your face
Go down again and turn to nothingness

SIRIUSBEGLEITER

Von den Dingen, die ich sah
bist du mir besonders nah

Fühle aller Welten Schluß
Was da kommen wird und muß

Ein vollkommner Diamant
Hast du Raum und Zeit verbrannt

Deiner ungeheuren Schwere
Bleibt allein der Weg ins Leere

Dein dir anvertrautes Leben
hast du wieder weggegeben

Erdenkleiner Sternengreis
Heiß wie Feuer, weiß wie Eis

Deine Härte ist der Tod
Unsrer Herzen, der uns droht

SIRIUS'S COMPANION

Of the things I saw
you're closest to me

Feel the end of all worlds
What's coming and must

A perfect diamond
You burnt time and space

What remains is your incredible
Weight's path into the void

You gave it away again
your own life entrusted to you

Earthly-small red giant
Hot like fire, white like ice

Your toughness is the impending
Death of our hearts

ELEKTRONISCHE HIRNE

Noch sind sie unsere Knechte
Noch führen sie aus
Was wir ihnen vorschreiben
Dumm, stur, emsig

Aber schon sind die Resultate
Die sie liefern
Nicht mehr zu kontrollieren
Nur durch ihresgleichen

Doch bald
Werden sie weiter rechnen
Ohne uns
Formeln finden,
die nicht mehr zu interpretieren sind

Bis sie endlich Gott erkennen,
ohne ihn zu verstehen
Schuld- und erbarmungslos
Straf- und rostfrei
Gefallene Engel

ELECTRIC BRAINS

They're still our servants
They still perform
What we command
Dumb, stubborn, diligent

But already the results
They deliver
Are uncontrollable
Except for the likes of them

And soon
They'll continue to calculate
Without us
Find formulas
that are no longer interpretable

Until they finally detect God,
without understanding Him
Innocent and merciless
Unpunished and rust free
Fallen angels

EIN PSALM SALOMOS, DEN WELTRAUMFAHRERN ZU SINGEN

Aus der Komödie DIE PHYSIKER

Wir hauten ins Weltall ab.
Zu den Wüsten des Monds. Versanken in ihrem Staub.
Lautlos verreckten
Manche schon da. Doch die meisten verkochten
In den Bleidämpfen des Merkurs, lösten sich auf
In den Ölpfützen der Venus, und
Sogar auf dem Mars fraß uns die Sonne,
Donnernd, radioaktiv und gelb.

Jupiter stank
Ein pfeilschnell rotierender Methanbrei,
Hing er so mächtig über uns,
Daß wir Ganymed vollkotzten.

Saturn bedachten wir mit Flüchen.
Was dann weiter kam, nicht der Rede wert:
Uranus, Neptun
Graugrünlich erfroren,
Über Pluto und Transpluto fielen die letzten
Unanständigen Witze.

Hatten wir doch längst die Sonne mit Sirius verwechselt
Sirius mit Kanopus,
Abgetrieben trieben wir in die Tiefen hinauf
Einigen weißen Sternen zu,
Die wir gleichwohl nie erreichten,
Längst schon Mumien in unseren Schiffen
Verkrustet von Unrat:
In den Fratzen kein Erinnern mehr
An die atmende Erde.

A SOLOMONIC PSALM, TO BE SUNG TO ASTRONAUTS

From the comedy THE PHYSICISTS

We took off into the universe.
To the moon's deserts. Drowned in their dust.
Many croaked without a sound
There already. But most of them boiled to shreds
In Mercury's lead fumes, disintegrated
In Venus's oil puddles, and
The sun devoured us even on Mars,
Thundering, radioactive and yellow.

Jupiter stank
A fast-rotating mash of methane,
It hung so mightily above us
That we puked all over Ganymede.

We covered Saturn with curses.
What came next is not worth mentioning:
Uranus, Neptune
Frozen gray-green,
Over Pluto and Transpluto fell
The last dirty jokes.

We'd long mistaken Sirius for the sun
Sirius for Canopus,
Off course, we drifted up into the depths
Towards a few white stars
We would never reach anyway,
Already mummies in our ships
Covered in crusted filth:
There were no memories left in our grimaces
Of the breathing world.

LIED

Ich zog durch Wüsten, stieg
    nieder in Wälder
sah Ninive liegen, sah Ur
    die Steppe von Tartar
und den Henker, zum Kuckuck
    beschmiert mit eurem Blut

Ich achtete nicht seiner
Ich wußte, ich würde entkommen
    und ich entkam.

Werde Denker, zum Kuckuck
    bewahre den Mut
Kenne dich selber

Ich zog durch Wüsten wieder, stieg
    nieder in Wälder wieder
sah Ninive aufs neue, doch darnieder
Ur verbrannt, die Steppe von Tartar
    voll Rauch
und den Henker, zum Kuckuck
    beschmiert mit meinem Blut
Denn der Henker kannte mich auch

Ich achtete nicht seiner
Ich wußte, ich würde entkommen
    und ich entkam
nicht ein zweites Mal

SONG

I roamed through deserts, climbed
    down into forests
saw Nineveh lying, saw Ur
    the Tartar Steppe
and the executioner, for crying out loud
    besmeared with your blood

I didn't pay attention to him
I knew I would escape
    and I did.

Become a thinker, for crying out loud
    keep courage
Know yourself

I roamed through deserts again, climbed
    down into forests,
saw Nineveh anew, but below
Ur was burnt, the Tartar Steppe
    full of smoke
and the executioner, for crying out loud
    besmeared with my blood
For the executioner knew me, too

I didn't pay attention to him
I knew I would escape
    and I did
but not twice

DIE MAKAMEN DES BETTLERS AKKI

Aus der Komödie EIN ENGEL KOMMT NACH BABYLON

So hört die Makame meines Lebens: In jungen Jahren, vor viel tausend Jahren, wie ich unerfahren, war ich eines Kaufmanns Sohn. Mein Vater in goldenem Kleide, meine Mutter in Silbergeschmeide, das Haus voll Teppich, Sammet und Seide. Das Silber wird schwarz, das Gold rollt davon, da rollte es schon: In Babylon fraß alles die Firma Enggibi und Sohn. Schon brannte der Vater, die Mutter schon, auf der Scheiterbeige, es kam keiner davon.

Ein Prophet kam, aus dem Bergland Elam, der mich zu sich nahm; und er hielt mich wie einen Sohn. Lag Tag und Nacht vor dem Altar, brachte den Göttern Opfer dar, in Fetzen gehüllt und Asche im Haar. Die Religion wird schwarz, die Gnad' rollt davon, da rollte sie schon: In Babylon wechselte der Priesterthron. Schon brannte der Prophet, die Götter schon, auf der Scheiterbeige, es kam keiner davon.

Der mich nun aufzog, war General, gepanzert in Eisen, bewaffnet mit Stahl, und tat getreu, was der König befahl; nie war geehrter einer Mutter Sohn. Stach den Feind vom Roß, besaß ein Schloß, unermeßlich war sein rasselnder Troß. Die Ehre wird schwarz, das Amt rollt davon, da rollte es schon: In Babylon wechselte der Königsthron. Schon brannte der General, die Knappen schon, auf der Scheiterbeige, es kam keiner davon.

Wie der Reiche verdarb und der Fromme starb, und auch der Starke den Tod erwarb, sagte sich meiner Mutter Sohn: Der Mensch sei wie Sand, Sand allein hält stand den Tritten der Schächer, der Henker im Land. Die Zeit wird schwarz, die Macht rollt davon, laß rollen sie schon: Von Babylon bleibt nur ein Bettler, bekränzt mit Mohn, und brennt sein Bart, sein Mantel schon, auf der Scheiterbeige, er kommt davon.

So hört die Makame meiner erbettelten Berufe. In der Blütenpracht einer Maiennacht, um Mitternacht, erbettelte ich mit Kunst und Schlich von einem Milliardärstöchterlein seines Papas Milliarde ein. Unverdrossen, war ich entschlossen, in einem Kampf auf Brechen und Biegen, den frechen Dampf des Reichtums zu

THE MAQAMAT OF AKKI THE BEGGAR

From the comedy AN ANGEL COMES TO BABYLON

So hear my life's maqam: In younger years, many thousand years ago, inexperienced, I was a merchant's son. My father in golden robes, my mother in ornaments, the house full of rugs, samet and silk. The silver turns black, the gold rolls away, there it rolled already: In Babylon, the firm Enggibi and Son devoured everything. Already the father was burning, already the mother, on the funeral pyre, nobody got away.

A prophet came from the mountainous country of Elam, took me in, and cared for me as if for his own son. Day and night he lay in front of the altar, made sacrifices to the gods, draped in rags with ashes in his hair. Religion turns black, mercy rolls away, there it rolled already: In Babylon, the priest's throne changed hands. Already the prophet was burning, already the gods, on the funeral pyre, nobody got away.

He who cared for me now was a general, clad with iron, armed with blade, who followed faithfully the king's orders; no mother's son was ever more honored. He stabbed the enemy off his horse, owned a castle, and immense was his rattling caravan. Honor turns black, duty rolls away, there it rolled already: In Babylon, the king's throne changed hands. Already the general was burning, already the varlets, on the funeral pyre, nobody got away.

As the rich one was undone and the pious one expired, and as the strong one earned his death, my mother's son said to himself: Man is like sand, sand alone withstands the muggers' kicks, the hangmen of the land. Time turns black, power rolls away, let it roll already: Of Babylon only a beggar remains, crowned with poppy, and even though his beard is burning, his coat, on the funeral pyre, he gets away.

So hear the maqam of my begged trades. In the bloom of a night in May, at midnight, I begged with trick and fake daddy's billions from his young billionaire daughter. Undaunted, I was determined to defeat the brazen vapor of wealth, in a battle of make or break. Hear now what the wise one did: From dawn till dusk I ran into

besiegen. Höre nun, was der Weise tat: Früh bis spat machte ich Schulden, vertrank die Gulden, verstank die Wälder und Schlösser, die Kälber und Rösser, verspielte selber die Kunstgegenstände, die goldenen Spiegel, die Tiegel, die Wände, verpraßte die Schreine, verschaßte die Steine, verjaßte alleine zweitausend Schweine, und so, in unwiderstehlichem Trott, war ich in einem Jahr bankerott, ganz und gar, ohne Sou in der Tasche, ohne Wein in der Flasche, und im gleichen liederlichen Tritt zog ich weitere fünf Milliardäre mit, samt Aktionären und Banken; das Land kam ins Wanken. Dies, mein Henker, tat ich als Denker, um einen bösen Beruf zu erlösen.

Da ich nun in meinem Sarkophag Nacht und Tag denkend lag, warum die Menschheit in Krämpfen liege, warum Gemeinheit im Kämpfen siege, suchte ich mit Geisteskraft und Feuer, meiner Leidenschaft ein neues Abenteuer: Mit Hoftieren und Scharmieren, mit Malträtieren und Exerzieren, mit Arschlecken und Rückenverrenken, mit Beinestrecken und patriotischem Denken, mit aristokratischer Braut und bürokratischem Laut, mit Wedeln und Kriechen, erbettelte ich von einem siechen General den Titel. Nun hatte ich Mittel, den Krieg zu bekriegen, und den Sieg zu besiegen. Dies war der Sinn meines militärischen Lebens, die Höllenfahrt war nicht vergebens. Ich erreichte mit kühnen Systemen, dem Krieg die Mühen und Schrecken zu nehmen. Als die Armee, die ich führte, nach Akkad marschierte, dreihunderttausend auf dem Papier, gelang es mir, die Schlacht zu verlieren, ohne einen Toten nach Hause zu führen, ohne Wunden, unzerschunden, ohne Verluste an Menschen und Tieren. Keine Mutter verlor ihren Sohn, dreihunderttausend kamen davon. Dies, mein Henker, des Denkers Spruch: Nie gab's einen billigeren Zusammenbruch!

Die Welt zu bestehen, muß der Schwache sie erkennen, um nicht blind einen Weg zu gehen, der sich verliert, in eine Gefahr zu rennen, die zum Tode führt. Die Mächtigen sind mächtig; es ist niederträchtig, diese Wahrheit zu mißachten, nach Narrheit zu trachten, die Mächtigen zu besiegen, ohne über Waffen zu verfügen, denen sie unterliegen. Heldentaten sind sinnlos, sie verraten die Ohnmacht des Schwachen, und seine Verzweiflung bringt die Macht nur zum Lachen. Doch hört einen Bettler jetzt, gefoltert, in Fetzen, von Schergen gehetzt: Der Mächtige in dieser Welt greift nach dem, was ihm gefällt, bald ist es dein Weib, bald

debt, drank away the guilders, sullied the forests and castles, calves and horses, gambled away the art collection, the golden mirrors, the pots and pans, the walls, squandered the shrines, frittered away the precious stones, lost two thousand pigs in a game of cards alone, and thus, stuck in my irresistible rut, I was bankrupt within a year, completely, without a sou in my pocket, without wine in my bottle, and with the same rakish step I took along another five billionaires, stockholders, banks, and all; the land began to totter. This, my hangman, I did as a thinker, to deliver an evil trade.

Lying in my sarcophagus, night and day, thinking of why mankind lies cramping, why mean tricks win battles, I sought with strength of mind and fire a new adventure for my passion: With farm animals and sweet talk, with maltreatment and exercise, with brownnosing and back-straining, with leg-stretching and patriotic thinking, with an aristocratic bride and bureaucratic noise, with wagging and creeping, I begged the title from a wasted general. Now I had the means to fight war and to defeat victory. This was the object of my military existence, the hellish ride was not made in vain. With bold systems I accomplished to rid war of its horror and pain. When the army I led marched on Akkad, three hundred thousand strong on paper, I succeeded to lose the battle, without leading home one dead, without wounds, unblemished, without any loss of man or beast. No mother lost her son, three hundred thousand got away. This, my hangman, is the thinker's verdict: There's never been a cheaper collapse.

To survive the world, the weak one must realize it, so as not to follow blindly a path that loses itself, running into danger, leading to death. The mighty are mighty; it's wicked to ignore this truth, to be looking for folly, to defeat the mighty without access to arms they must be defeated by. Heroic deeds are futile, they give away the weak's powerlessness, and their despair just brings laughter to the mighty. But now listen to a beggar, tortured, in rags, baited by myrmidons: The mighty one in this world grabs what he likes, soon it will be your woman, soon it will be your house, and only what he despises he leaves untouched; the bright one shall learn from this. He falls who's seduced by what might desires, violence kills even the wise, only who has nothing and is nothing remains safe. Understand what one must, and then draw your conclusion: Play stupid, that's the only way you'll grow old. Attack from the

ist es dein Haus, und nur, was er verachtet, läßt er unberührt; es lerne der Kluge daraus. Der fällt, den verführt, was die Macht begehrt, ja selbst den Weisen tötet die Gewalt, nur wer nichts hat und nichts ist, bleibt unversehrt. Begreife, was man muß, und ziehe den Schluß: Stelle dich dumm, nur so wirst du alt. Von innen greife an. Sei in der Festung schon am Tage des Gerichts. Schleiche dich ein, demütigen Gesichts, als Saufkumpan, als Sklave, Dichter, Schuldenbauer, erniedrige dich, und du brichst jede Mauer. Ertrage Schmach, geh jede Pfade, vergrabe, will's die Zeit, wilde Hoffnung, heiße Liebe, Leid und Gnade, Menschlichkeit, unter einem roten Henkerskleid.

inside. Be already within the castle walls on Judgment Day. Sneak inside, with a humble face, as drinking buddy, as slave, poet, debt builder, humiliate yourself, and you will break through any wall. Bear disgrace, walk every path, bury, if you want time, wild hope, hot love, suffering and mercy, and humanity under a red hangman's dress.

DAS UNVERMEIDLICHE WARTET

Das Unvermeidliche wartet
Es kommt nicht. Du kommst
Die Maus bist Du. Darum
Sei kein Held
Denn dem Furchtlosen
Ist auch das Vermeidliche
Unvermeidlich
Fürchte Dich. Bleib ein Mensch
Was Dir gehört, gehört Dir nicht
Was allen gehört, gehört Dir
Die richtigen Gedanken
Sie sind freundlich
Auch wenn sie feindlich scheinen
Du kannst sie nicht allein denken
Du kannst sie nicht allein überprüfen
Du kommst nicht allein auf sie
Allein vor sie kommst Du allein
Sie sind Deine und unsere Richter
Wir sind falsch und Du, nicht sie
Liebe ihr Urteil, wende es an
Vielleicht wird dann das dunkle Tier
Sich räkelnd unter einem Bett
Oder schnurrend an einer Straße geduckt
Sein unmenschliches Tagwerk
Menschlich verrichten
Dich nicht
In einer Gaskammer fressen

THE INEVITABLE WAITS

The inevitable waits
It's not coming. You are
You are the mouse. So
Don't be a hero
When for the fearless
Even the avoidable
Is unavoidable
Fear. Stay human
What belongs to you, doesn't
What belongs to all, does
The right thoughts
They are friendly
Even when they seem hostile
You cannot think them alone
You cannot check them alone
You don't strike on them alone
Alone you appear in front of them alone
They are your judges and ours
We are wrong and you, not they
Love their verdict, use it
Perhaps then the dark animal
Lolling under a bed
Or purring, crouched by a street
Will perform humanely
Its inhuman day's work
And not devour you
In a gas chamber

NUR DAS NICHTIGE HAT BESTAND

Wütend und naß
glitt ich aus dem Leib meiner Mutter
begriff nie wozu
und auf wessen Befehl
später blinzelte ich im Licht
und wurde mißtrauisch
so bin ich immer noch
genüge mir selber; die Welt
da draußen
ist ungewiß. Sie gehört nicht mir.
Ist eine unbegreifliche Gnade
oder auch
ein böser Fluch. Wer kann das
wissen
Auf alles gefaßt sein.
Darum sammle ich die Weine
rauche die braunen getrockneten
Blätter
Vergänglichkeit
nur das Nichtige hat
Bestand.

ONLY NOTHINGNESS STANDS

Furious and wet
            I slid out of my mother's body
      without ever knowing why
or on whose order
      I later blinked in the light
                        and became distrustful
so I am still
      satisfied with myself; the world
outside
      is uncertain. It doesn't belong to me.
It's an incomprehensible mercy
      or
an evil curse. Who
                                                knows
To be prepared for anything.
            That's why I collect the bottles of wine
smoke the dried brown
                        leaves
Transience
                  only nothingness
            stands.

ERGREIFE DIE FEDER MÜDE

Ergreife die Feder müde
schreibe deine Gedanken nieder
    wenn keine Frage nach Stil dich bedrängt.

Es ist heute wieder vieles zu durchdenken.
Felder liegen brach, die einst Früchte trugen.

Das Mögliche ist ungeheuer. Die Sucht
    nach Perfektion
zerstört das meiste. Was bleibt
    sind Splitter
an denen sinnlos gefeilt wurde.

Beginne, das Sonnensystem zu sehen.
    Liebe
auch Pluto. Doch wer
    macht sich schon Gedanken über ihn!
Ich aber
    spüre sein Kreisen, ahne
die kleine Kugel, die glattgeschliffene.

Alles läßt sich besser schreiben
    Darum laß die schlechtere Fassung stehn.

Nur beim Weitergehen kommst du irgendwohin
    wohin?
Fern von dir.
    Gehe weiter. Lots Weib
erstarrte beim Zurückschauen.
    Erstarrt nicht. Korrigiert nicht.
Wagt!

Höre nie auf andere.
Trachte nicht danach ein gutes Buch zu schreiben
Mache keinen Plan und wenn du ihn machst
    führe ihn nicht aus
Der Plan genügt.

WHEN YOU'RE TIRED, PICK UP THE PEN

When you're tired, pick up the pen
write down your thoughts
    when you're not pressed by questions of style.

Today much needs to be thought through.
Fields that once bore fruit lie fallow.

The possible is monstrous. The addiction
    to perfection
destroys most things. What remains
    are splinters
that have been filed at needlessly.

Begin to see the solar system.
    Love
even Pluto. But who
    cares about him?
I however
    feel his circling, sense
this small globe, sanded smoothly.

Everything can be written better
    So keep the inferior draft.

Only when keep moving will you get somewhere
    where?
Far away from you.
    Keep moving. Lot's woman
froze when she looked back.
    Don't freeze. Don't revise.
Dare!

Never listen to others.
Never aspire to write a good book
Don't make a plan, and if you do
    don't follow it
The plan's enough.

Nichts
    ist notwendig. Das Spiel
kann jederzeit abgebrochen werden.

Es gibt Sätze, die stark machen
    doch brauchen sie nicht niedergeschrieben
    werden

Löse deine Hand.

Es kommt nie auf die Sätze an. Nur das
Werk allein zählt.
    Die Narren kritisieren einen Satz
Wenige sehen das Ganze

    Gott kann dich verlassen
    Gody soll dich verlassen.

Nothing
    is necessary. The game
can be abandoned at any time.

There are sentences that empower
    but they don't need to be
    written down

Free your hand.

It's never about sentences. Only the
Work counts.
    Fools criticize a sentence
Few see the whole thing

    God can abandon you
    Gody shall abandon you.

DER MENSCHEN KETTEN LOSZUKETTEN

»Lied der Marxe« aus der Komödie ACHTERLOO IV

Der Menschen Ketten loszuketten
Erschufen wir die Ketten neu
Weil Menschen hoffen nur in Ketten
Daß kettenlos die Zukunft sei

Nur wer gekettet ist in Ketten
Der weiß wie schwer die Kette wiegt
Daß ihn von Ketten nur wird retten
Was in der Zukunft Kette liegt

So an die Hoffnung angekettet
Sind wir auf Ketten stolz wie nie
Gekettet sind wir losgekettet
An eine neue Utopie

TO UNCHAIN MAN'S CHAINS

"*Song of the Marxs*" *from the comedy* ACHTERLOO IV

To unchain man's chains
We created the chain anew
Only chained does man believe
In a future without chains

Only he who's chained
Knows the chain's weight
That only what's to be chained
Will save him from chains

Thus chained to hope, of chains
We've never been more proud
Unchained we are chained
To a new Utopia

MINOTAURUS

Für Charlotte

Das Wesen, das die Tochter des Sonnengottes,
Pasiphae, geboren hatte, nachdem sie auf ihren
Wunsch hin eingeschlossen in eine künstliche Kuh
von einem dem Poseidon geweihten weißen Stier
bestiegen worden war, fand sich, von den
Knechten des Minos hineingeschleppt, die lange
Ketten bildeten, um sich nicht zu verlieren, nach
langen Jahren eines wirren Schlafs, währenddessen
es in einem Stall zwischen Kühen heranwuchs,
auf dem Boden des Labyrinths vor, das von
Daidalos erbaut worden war, um die Menschen
vor dem Wesen und das Wesen vor den
Menschen zu schützen, einer Anlage, aus der
keiner, der sie betreten hatte, wieder herausfand
und deren unzählige in sich verschachtelte Wände
aus Glas waren, so daß das Wesen nicht nur seinem
Spiegelbild gegenüberkauerte, sondern auch
den Spiegelbildern seiner Spiegelbilder: Es sah
unermeßlich viele Wesen, wie es eines war, vor sich,
und wie es sich herumdrehte, um sie nicht
mehr zu sehen, unermeßlich viele ihm gleiche
Wesen wiederum vor sich. Es befand sich in
einer Welt voll kauernder Wesen, ohne zu wissen,
daß es selber das Wesen war. Es war wie gelähmt.
Es wußte nicht, wo es war, noch was die kauernden
Wesen rundherum wollten, vielleicht träumte
es nur, auch wenn es nicht wußte, was Traum war
und was Wirklichkeit. Es sprang auf, instinktiv,
um die kauernden Wesen zu vertreiben, gleichzeitig
sprangen seine Spiegelbilder auf. Es duckte
sich, und mit ihm duckten sich seine Spiegelbilder.
Sie ließen sich nicht vertreiben. Es starrte auf
das Spiegelbild, das ihm am nächsten schien, kroch
langsam zurück, und auch sein Spiegelbild
wich von ihm weg, sein rechter Fuß stieß an
eine Wand, es warf sich herum und fand sich Kopf
an Kopf mit seinem Spiegelbild, kroch vorsichtig

THE MINOTAUR

For Charlotte

The creature, born to Pasiphae,
daughter of the Sun god, who,
at her own wish, had been locked
into a false cow and mounted by
Poseidon's blesséd White Bull,
found himself dragged in by Mino's
servants, who forged long chains,
so as not to run out, after many years
of a reeling sleep of growing up
among cows in a stable, on the floor
of Daedalus's labyrinth built to protect
men from the creature and the creature
from men, a floor plan from which
no one who entered found a way out
and whose countless interlaced walls
were made of glass, so that the creature
not only cowered facing his own reflection
but the reflections of his reflections: He
saw an uncountable number of creatures
like him before him, and when he turned
around to avoid them, he faced again an
uncountable number of creatures like him.
He was in a world filled with cowering
creatures, without knowing that he himself
was the creature. He was almost numb.
He didn't know where he was or what
the cowering creatures around him wanted,
perhaps he was only dreaming, even though
he didn't know what a dream was, what reality
was. He jumped up, instinctively, to drive
away the cowering creatures, at the same
time, his reflections jumped up. He ducked,
and his reflections with him. They refused
to be driven away. He stared at the reflection
closest to him, slowly crept away, and his
reflection crept away from him, his right foot
bumped into a wall, he flung himself around

zurück, sein Spiegelbild kroch zurück. Unwillkürlich betastete es seinen Kopf, und wie es ihn betastete, betasteten auch seine Spiegelbilder ihren Kopf. Es erhob sich, und mit ihm erhoben sich auch seine Spiegelbilder. Es sah seinen Leib hinunter und verglich ihn mit dem Leib seiner Spiegelbilder, und seine Spiegelbilder sahen ihren Leib hinunter und verglichen ihn mit ihrem Leib, und indem es sich und seine Spiegelbilder betrachtete, erkannte es, daß es wie seine Spiegelbilder beschaffen war: Es glaubte, ein Wesen unter vielen gleichen Wesen zu sein. Sein Gesicht wurde freundlicher, die Gesichter seiner Spiegelbilder wurden freundlicher. Es winkte ihnen zu, sie winkten zurück, es winkte mit der rechten, sie winkten mit der linken Hand, aber es wußte weder was rechts noch was links war. Es reckte sich, streckte die Arme aus, brüllte, mit ihm reckte sich, streckte die Arme aus und brüllte eine Unzahl gleicher Wesen, tausendfach scholl sein Echo zurück, schien endlos zu brüllen. Ein Glücksgefühl überkam es. Es näherte sich der nächsten Wand aus Glas, ein Spiegelbild näherte sich ihm ebenfalls, während gleichzeitig sich andere Spiegelbilder entfernten. Es berührte sein Spiegelbild mit der Rechten, berührte die Linke seines Spiegelbilds, die sich glatt und kalt anfühlte, vor ihm berührten sich in Spiegelbildern von Spiegelbildern die anderen Spiegelbilder. Es lief, den glatten Spiegel berührend, die Wand entlang, seine rechte Hand die linke seines Spiegelbilds deckend, mit ihm lief sein Spiegelbild, und wie es nun die Rückseite der Spiegelwand zurücklief, lief sein Spiegelbild auch zurück. Es wurde übermütiger, sprang herum, überschlug sich, und mit ihm sprang und überschlug sich eine Unermeßlichkeit von Spiegelbildern. Aus dem Herumrennen und dem Sich-Überschlagen, aus den Sprüngen und dem Auf-den-Händen-Gehen—so groß wurde sein Übermut, weil die Spiegelbilder ja gleichzeitig dasselbe taten wie es, so daß es sich

and landed head-to-head with his reflection,
crept carefully backwards, his reflection
crept carefully backwards. He automatically
touched his head, and as he touched it,
his reflections touched their heads.
He stood up, and with him his reflections.
He saw down his body and compared it
to the body of his reflections, and his
reflections saw down their bodies
and compared them to their bodies,
and as he looked at himself and his reflections,
he realized that he resembled his reflections:
He believed to be one of many identical
beings. His face turned friendlier, the faces
of his reflections turned friendlier.
He waved to them, they waved back,
he waved with his right hand,
they waved with the left, but he didn't
know what was right and what was left.
He moved, stretched his arms, bellowed,
with him, a myriad of like beings moved,
stretched their arms, bellowed, a thousandfold
his echo hit back, and seemed to bellow
without end. A sense of happiness overcame
him. He approached the next glass wall,
a reflection came closer with him, while
at the same time other reflections moved
away. He touched his reflection with his right
hand, touched his reflection's left hand,
which felt smooth and cold, in front of him,
reflections touched the reflections of other
reflections. He ran along the wall, touching
the smooth mirror with his right hand, covering
the left hand of his reflection that ran with him,
and when he ran back along the other side
of the mirror, his reflection ran back with him.
He got excited, performed vaults and somersaults,
and with him vaulted, somersaulted an infinity
of reflections. From the running and somersaulting,
from the leaping and the handwalks,
his excitement became so great—

wie ein Anführer vorkam, mehr noch, wie ein Gott, wenn es gewußt hätte, was ein Gott ist—, aus dieser kindlichen Freude wurde allmählich ein rhythmischer Tanz des Wesens mit seinen Spiegelbildern, die teils spiegelverkehrt, teils als Spiegelbilder von Spiegelbildern mit dem Wesen identisch und wiederum als Spiegelbilder von Spiegelbildern von Spiegelbildern spiegelverkehrt waren, bis sie sich im Unendlichen verloren. Das Wesen tanzte durch sein Labyrinth, durch die Welt seiner Spiegelbilder, es tanzte wie ein monströses Kind, es tanzte wie ein monströser Vater seiner selbst, es tanzte wie ein monströser Gott durch das Weltall seiner Spiegelbilder. Doch plötzlich hielt es in seinem Tanz inne, stand starr, kauerte sich nieder, starrte mit aufmerksamen Augen, und mit ihm kauerten und äugten seine Spiegelbilder: Tanzend hatte das Wesen zwischen den tanzenden Spiegelbildern Wesen gesehen, die nicht tanzten und die keine Spiegelbilder waren, die ihm gehorchten. Das Mädchen, wie das kauernde Wesen widergespiegelt, stand unbeweglich, nackt, mit langen schwarzen Haaren zwischen den kauernden Wesen, die überall waren, vor ihm, neben ihm, hinter ihm, so wie es auch überall war, vor ihm, neben ihm, hinter ihm. Das Mädchen wagte sich nicht zu rühren, den angstvollen Blick auf das Wesen geheftet, das vor ihm kauerte und ihm am nächsten war. Es wußte, daß es nur ein kauerndes Wesen gab, daß die anderen kauernden Wesen Spiegelbilder waren, aber es wußte nicht, wer das Wesen und nicht sein Spiegelbild war. Vielleicht war es das Wesen, das vor ihm kauerte, vielleicht sein Spiegelbild, vielleicht ein Spiegelbild seines Spiegelbilds, das Mädchen wußte es nicht. Es wußte nur, daß seine Flucht vor ihm es zu ihm geführt hatte, und neben dem kauernden Wesen sah es sich selber gespiegelt, und weiter vor ihm sah es sich selber von hinten und neben sich ein kauerndes Wesen von hinten, und so fort durch endlose Räume. Die Hände

because the reflections kept on doing the same
things he did—that he felt like a leader, or more
like a god—had he known what a god was—
this childish joy grew slowly into a rhythmic
dance between the creature and his reflections
that were partly inverted, partly identical
with the creature as reflections of reflections,
and again inverted as reflections of reflections
of reflections, until they lost themselves in infinity.
The creature danced through his labyrinth,
through the world of his reflections, he danced
like a monstrous child, he danced like his monstrous
father, he danced like a monstrous god through
the universe of his reflections. But suddenly, he
stopped dead in his dance, stood stiff, cowered
down, stared with attentive eyes, and with him
cowered and stared his reflections:
Dancing, the creature had seen creatures
between his dancing reflections—they didn't dance,
and their reflections would not obey him. The girl,
reflected like the cowering creature, stood
fixed, naked, with long black hair, between
the cowering creatures that were everywhere,
in front of her, next to her, behind her,
just as she was everywhere, before her, next
to her, behind her. The girl didn't dare to move,
her anxious eyes fixed on the creature that
cowered before her and was closest to her.
She knew there was only one creature,
that the other cowering creatures were mere
reflections, but she didn't know which one
was creature and not reflection. Perhaps it was
the creature that cowered before her, perhaps
his reflection, perhaps a reflection of his reflection,
the girl didn't know. She only knew her flight from
him had led her to him, and she saw her
reflection next to the cowering creatures,
and farther ahead she saw herself from behind,
and next to her a cowering creature from behind,
and so forth, through endless spaces. With her
hands crossing her breasts, she watched, spellbound,

über die Brüste gekreuzt, sah es gebannt auf das immer noch vor ihm kauernde Wesen. Es glaubte, es berühren zu können. Es glaubte, seinen Atem zu spüren. Es glaubte, sein Schnauben zu hören. Sein gewaltiger, mit einem fahlen lichtbraunen Pelz bedeckter Kopf war der eines Auerochsen, die Stirn hoch, breit und von verfilzten Wollhaaren überwuchert, die Hörner kurz und so gebogen, daß die Spitzen über der Wurzel standen, die rötlichen Augen schienen eher klein im Verhältnis zum Schädel, und die Umrandung, in der sie lagen, war erhöht, die Augen waren unergründlich. Der sanft geneigte massige Nasenrücken führte zu schiefgestellten Nüstern, aus dem Maul hing eine lange bläulichrote Zunge und unter dem Kinn ein zopfiger geiferverklebter Bart. Dies alles wäre zu ertragen gewesen, aber das Unerträgliche war der Übergang dieses Bullen zum Menschen. Über dem Auerochsenschädel wölbte sich ein Gebirge von struppigem und dann wieder abgeschabtem Fell, aus dessen Grannen und Strähnen zwei Menschenarme wuchsen, die sich auf den gläsernen Boden stützten. Es war, als ob der ungeheure Kopf und der Buckel über ihm aus dem Leib eines Mannes gewuchert wären, der sprungbereit vor dem Mädchen kauerte und dann wieder neben und hinter ihm. Der Minotaurus erhob sich. Er war gewaltig. Er begriff plötzlich, daß es noch etwas anderes als Minotauren gab. Seine Welt hatte sich verdoppelt. Er sah die überall widergespiegelten Augen, den Mund, die langen schwarzen Haare, die über die Schultern flossen, er sah die weiße Haut, den Hals, die Brüste, den Bauch, den Schoß, die Schenkel, wie das alles ineinanderging, ineinanderfloß. Er bewegte sich zu ihm hin. Es entfernte sich von ihm, während es sich anderswo auf ihn zu bewegte. Er jagte ihm durch das Labyrinth nach, es flüchtete. Es war, als ob ein Sturmwind Minotauren und Mädchen durcheinandergeblasen hätte, so wirbelten sie auseinander, durcheinander und einander entgegen,

the still-cowering creature. She believed she could
touch him. She believed she could feel
his breath. She believed she could hear
his panting. His enormous head, covered
with a pale light-brown coat, was that of
an aurochs, the high forehead, wide and
overgrown with matted woolly hair,
horns short and so crooked their tips stood
right above their roots, the reddish eyes
seemed rather small compared to his skull,
and their sockets in which they lay were raised,
his eyes were bottomless. The softly slanted,
massive bridge of his nose led to misshapen
nostrils, from his mouth hung a bluish-red
tongue, and below the chin, a matted, slobbery
beard. All of this would've been bearable,
but the unbearable was the transition of bull
to man. A mountain of bristly and then scraped
hair arched over the aurochs's skull, from whose
awns and strands grew two human arms
that rested on the glass floor. It was as though
the tremendous head and the hump had grown
out of a man's body who cowered, ready
to leap, before the girl, and then again
next to and behind her. The Minotaur rose
to his feet. He was gigantic. He suddenly
realized that there were other things
than Minotaurs. His world had doubled.
He saw the everywhere reflected eyes,
the mouth, the long black hair that flowed
over her shoulders, he saw the white skin,
the neck, the breasts, the belly, the loins,
the thighs, how it all blended, flowed
into each other. He advanced towards her.
She backed away as she moved towards him
somewhere else. He chased her through
the labyrinth, she fled. It was as if a whirlwind
had jumbled together Minotaurs and girls,
this is how they whirled apart, together
and towards each other, and when the girl
ran into his arms, when he, all at once,

und als ihm das Mädchen in die Arme lief,
als er mit einem Male den Leib fühlte, das warme,
schweißgebadete Fleisch, und nicht das harte Glas,
das er bis jetzt gefühlt hatte, begriff er—insofern
man beim Minotaurus von Begreifen reden kann—,
daß er bis jetzt in einer Welt gelebt hatte,
in der es nur Minotauren gab, jeder eingeschlossen
in ein gläsernes Gefängnis, und nun fühlte
er einen anderen Leib, fühlte anderes Fleisch. Das
Mädchen entwand sich ihm, er ließ es geschehen.
Es wich zurück, die großen Augen auf ihn
gerichtet, und als er zu tanzen begann, begann
das Mädchen zu tanzen, und die Spiegelbilder der
beiden tanzten mit. Er tanzte seine Ungestalt,
es tanzte seine Schönheit, er tanzte seine Freude,
es gefunden zu haben, es tanzte seine Furcht, von
ihm gefunden worden zu sein, er tanzte seine Erlösung,
und es tanzte sein Schicksal, er tanzte seine
Gier, und es tanzte seine Neugier, er tanzte
sein Herandrängen, und es tanzte sein Abdrängen,
er tanzte sein Eindringen, es tanzte sein Umschlingen.
Sie tanzten, und ihre Spiegelbilder
tanzten, und er wußte nicht, daß er das Mädchen
nahm, er konnte auch nicht wissen, daß er es tötete,
wußte er doch nicht, was Leben war und was
Tod. In ihm war nichts als ein ungestümes Glück,
eins mit einer ungestümen Lust. Er brüllte auf,
als er das Mädchen nahm, und in den Spiegeln
nahmen Minotauren Mädchen, und das Brüllen
war ein ungeheuerlicher Schrei, ein unwirklicher
Weltschrei, als wäre nichts als dieser Schrei, der sich
mit dem Schrei des Mädchens vermischte,
und dann lag er da, und in den Spiegeln lagen
Minotauren da, und der weiße nackte Leib des
Mädchens mit den großen schwarzen Augen lag da
und spiegelte sich in den Wänden. Er hob den
linken Arm des Mädchens, er fiel herunter,
den rechten, er fiel herunter, überall fielen Arme
herunter. Er leckte es mit seiner bläulichroten
Riesenzunge, das Gesicht, die Brüste, das Mädchen
blieb unbeweglich, alle Mädchen blieben unbeweglich.

felt her body, the warm flesh dripping
with sweat, and not the hard glass
he'd felt until now, he realized--
insofar as one can talk of realization
when it comes to a Minotaur--that
until now, he had lived in a world
in which only Minotaurs existed, each
trapped in a glass prison, and now he felt
another body, felt other flesh. The girl
wrenched herself free of his grip, he
let it happen. She flinched, her large eyes
focusing on him, and when he began to
dance, the girl began to dance, and both
of their reflections danced along with them.
He danced his hideousness, she danced
her beauty, he danced the joy of having
found her, she danced the fear of having
been found by him, he danced his salvation,
and she danced her fate, he danced his lust,
and she danced her curiosity, he danced his
advance, and she danced her retreat, he
danced his penetration, and she danced
her embrace. They danced, and their
reflections danced, and he didn't know
that he took the girl, and he also didn't
know that he was killing her, for he didn't
know what life was, what death. Inside
of him was nothing but violent luck, one
with violent lust. He roared when he picked
up the girl, and in the mirrors, Minotaurs
picked up girls, and the roars were a monstrous
scream, an unreal scream of life, as if nothing
else existed but this scream that blended
with the scream of the girl, and then he lay
there, and in the mirrors lay Minotaurs, and
the girl's white, naked body with the large
black eyes lay there reflected in the walls. He
lifted her left arm, it fell, the right one, it
fell, arms fell everywhere. He licked her with
his giant bluish-red tongue, her face, her breasts,
but the girl remained lifeless, all the girls

Er wälzte es mit den Hörnern herum,
das Mädchen rührte sich nicht, kein Mädchen
rührte sich. Er erhob sich, sah sich um, überall
standen Minotauren und schauten sich um,
und überall lagen zu ihren Füßen weiße Mädchenleiber.
Er bückte sich, hob das Mädchen auf, brüllte,
klagte, hob das Mädchen dem dunklen Himmel
entgegen, und überall bückten sich Minotauren,
hoben Mädchen auf, brüllten, klagten, hoben
Mädchen dem dunklen Himmel entgegen, und
dann legte er das Mädchen zwischen die gläsernen
Wände, legte sich zu ihm und schlief ein,
und mit ihm alle Minotauren, hingestreckt auf dem
Boden voller weißer nackter Mädchenleiber.
Er schlief und träumte vom Mädchen mit den
schwarzen Haaren und den großen Augen, jagte
ihm nach, spielte mit ihm, riß es an sich, liebte es,
und als er die Augen öffnete, war auf seiner Brust
etwas in seinem verkrusteten Bart verkrallt.
Es streifte mit seinen Schwingen sein Flotzmaul
und tauchte seinen nackten gelblichweißen Hals mit
dem kleinen Kopf, den roten Augen und dem
seltsam gebogenen mächtigen Schnabel irgendwohin
neben ihm hinab. Auf den Wänden hockte
ein fettes Dickicht von Federn, Hälsen, Augen,
Schnäbeln, und über ihm kreiste es, den aufgrauenden
Morgen verfinsternd, stieß herab, tauchte,
riß, weidete, fledderte, wühlte, fraß, kreischte,
flog davon, flog heran, stieß wieder herab,
spiegelte sich im Herabfallen und im Hinaufsteigen,
ohne daß er begriff, warum es herabstieß,
hineintauchte, riß, hinaufstieg, herumkreiste,
so sehr war er eingehüllt vom Geflatter und
Flügelschlagen, und als es sich, immer höher
kreisend, im überhellen Nichts des nun gleißenden
Himmels auflöste, brach die Sonne durch die
gläsernen Wände und brannte ihr Bild in sein Hirn
als ein gewaltiges, sich drehendes Rad, das Feuergarben
in den Himmel stieß zum Zeichen ihres
Zorns über den Frevel ihrer Tochter Pasiphae, die
ein Wesen geboren hatte, das, eine Beleidigung

remained lifeless. He rolled her around
with his horns, the girl didn't move,
not one girl moved. He got up, looked around,
Minotaurs stood everywhere, looking
around, and everywhere the girls' white
bodies lay at their feet. He bent down,
picked up the girl, roared, moaned,
lifted the girl towards the dark sky,
and everywhere Minotaurs bent down,
picked up girls, roared, moaned, lifted
girls towards the dark sky, and then he
put the girl between the glass walls,
lay beside her, and fell asleep, and
with him all Minotaurs, lying prone
on the ground full of the girls' white,
naked bodies. He slept and dreamt
of the girl with the black hair and
the large eyes, chasing her, playing with her,
grabbing her, loving her, and when he opened
his eyes, there was something on his
chest, digging its claws into his crusty
beard. It brushed his muzzle with its
wings and plunged its naked, yellowish-white
neck and small head, the red eyes
and the strangely mighty beak, somewhere
into his side. On the walls sat a fat mass
of feathers, necks, eyes, beaks, and it
circled above him, darkening the dawn,
plunged, dove, ripped, grazed, fluttered,
dug, gorged, screeched, flew away, flew back,
plunged down again, reflections of its fall
and rise, without his understanding as to why
it plunged down, dug in, ripped, rose, circled,
he was enshrouded by wings flapping and stroking,
and as it circled ever higher, dissolving into the
overly bright nothingness of the by now blazing
sky, the sun broke through the glass walls and
burnt its picture into his brain as a giant turning
wheel tossing sheaves of fire into the sky as a
sign of its fury over daughter Pasiphae's sacrilege,
who'd given birth to a creature that, as an offense

der Götter und ein Fluch den Menschen, verdammt war, weder Gott noch Mensch noch Tier, sondern nur Minotaurus zu sein, schuldlos und schuldig zugleich. Er sah das unermeßliche, sich hinaufwälzende Rad, er hielt die Augen geschlossen, er sah es dennoch, das Rad des Fluches, der auf ihm lastete, das Rad seines Geschicks, das Rad seiner Geburt und das Rad seines Todes, das Rad, das in seinem Hirn brannte, ohne daß er wußte, was Fluch, Geschick, Geburt und Tod war, das Rad, das sich über ihn wälzte, das Rad, worin er gerädert war, und wie er dalag, versengt von der Sonne und von ihrem endlos widergespiegelten Licht, bemerkte er schattenhaft einen Fuß, der seinem Fuß glich. Er dachte, es sei das Mädchen, es sei wieder beweglich geworden und wolle mit ihm spielen. Er hob seinen Kopf, und nun sah er zwei Füße, die zurückwichen. Er erhob sich. Vor ihm stand ein Wesen, das dem Mädchen glich und doch nicht das Mädchen war, das in der Linken einen zerfetzten Mantel und in der Rechten ein Schwert hielt, und der Minotaurus wußte weder, was ein Mantel noch was ein Schwert war, er wußte nur—weil im blendenden Licht der Sonne die Wände kein Bild mehr zurückwarfen—, daß die Minotauren und die Mädchen ihn verlassen hatten, und auch das Mädchen, das er genommen hatte, mußte wieder beweglich geworden und fortgegangen sein, war es doch nicht mehr da. Er war ausgestoßen aus seiner Minotaurenwelt, allein mit dem Wesen, das, ihn beobachtend, zurückwich, stehenblieb, ihm entgegenging und wieder zurückwich. Der Minotaurus näherte sich ihm voll Wohlwollen, auch wenn er keinen Begriff für dieses Gefühl hatte, das anders war als jenes, das er dem Mädchen gegenüber gehabt hatte, weniger jäh, weniger gierig. Er freute sich, mit ihm in den Gängen zu spielen und zu jagen, vielleicht würde das Wesen ihn zu den anderen Minotauren führen und zu den Mädchen und zu den Wesen, die so waren wie dieses neue Wesen.

to the gods and a curse of man, was damned
to be not god, not man, not animal, but simply
Minotaur, at once innocent and guilty. He
saw the immense rolling wheel, he kept his
eyes closed, but still saw it, the wheel
of curses that weighed on him, the wheel
of his destiny, the wheel of his birth
and the wheel of his death, the wheel
that was burning in his brain, without
knowing the meaning of curse, destiny, birth
and death, the wheel that rolled over him,
the wheel on which he was broken, and as he lay
there, charred by the sun and its endlessly reflected
light, he noticed a foot among the shadows,
a foot that resembled his. He thought it was
the girl, he thought she'd come back to life
and wanted to play with him. He lifted his head,
and now he saw two feet retreating. He got up.
Before him stood a creature that resembled the girl
but wasn't the girl, that carried a tattered cape
in its left hand and a sword in its right, and
the Minotaur didn't know what a cape was
or what a sword was, he only knew—
because, in the sun's blinding light, the walls
no longer cast any reflections—that the Minotaurs
and the girls had left him, even the girl
he'd taken must've come back to life and left,
for she was no longer there. He was expelled
from his world of Minotaurs, alone with
the creature that, watching him, stepped back,
stood still, walked towards and away
from him. Full of good will, the Minotaur
approached it, even though he had no
concept of good will, which was much
different from what he'd felt for the girl,
less sudden, less voracious. He was happy
to be playing and chasing through the corridors,
perhaps the creature would lead him
to the other Minotaurs and to the girls
and to the creatures that were like this
new one. But he had to be more careful,

Nur mußte er mit ihm sorgfältiger umgehen,
zärtlicher, sonst würde es unbeweglich.
Der Minotaurus schnaubte freudig, und als das Wesen
wieder den Mantel schwenkte, begann er zu tanzen.
Vor den im Sonnenlicht strahlenden Wänden
bewegten sich die beiden wie Schatten, der tanzende
und springende, in die Hände klatschende
und dann wieder schnell stampfende Minotaurus,
das sein Tuch schwenkende, vorrückende oder
zurückweichende Wesen, immer wieder mit dem
Schwert angreifend, das es unter dem Mantel
verborgen ins Labyrinth mitgenommen hatte, den
Minotaurus zu töten, und nun, wie es ihm gegenüberstand
und es seine Arglosigkeit sah, schämte
es sich. Der Minotaurus umtanzte es, umklatschte
und umstampfte es. Er tanzte seine Freude, nicht
mehr allein zu sein, er tanzte seine Hoffnung,
die anderen Minotauren zu treffen, die Mädchen
und Wesen, die gleich waren wie jenes, mit dem er
nun tanzte. Er vergaß im Tanzen die Sonne,
er vergaß im Tanzen den Fluch. Er war nur noch
Heiterkeit, Freundlichkeit, Leichtigkeit, Zärtlichkeit.
Er tanzte, und das Wesen umlauerte und
umsprang den Minotaurus, und als die Sonne sank,
wurden mit ihrem tausendfachen Spiegelbild
auch die Spiegelbilder der beiden sichtbar.
Der Minotaurus tanzte, glücklich, die Minotauren
gefunden zu haben und die neuen Wesen, bald
würde er das Mädchen finden, das er genommen
hatte und das unbeweglich geworden und
das dann fortgegangen war, und die anderen
Mädchen, die von den Minotauren genommen
worden waren und dann auch unbeweglich
geworden und fortgegangen waren. Die beiden
tanzten einander entgegen und tanzten einander
auseinander, die Spiegelbilder trafen sich, deckten
sich, durchschossen sich. Überall tanzte ein
Minotaurus herum, drehte sich um sich selber,
und überall sprang der Jüngling vor und sprang
wieder zurück, federnd, dann wieder in Bocksprüngen,
darauf wartend zuzustoßen, und als die Sonne

more tender, otherwise, it would become lifeless. The Minotaur snorted with joy, and when the creature swung its cape again, he began to dance. In front of the walls radiating with sunlight, the two of them moved like shadows, the dancing and jumping, the clapping and then again fast-stamping Minotaur, the cape-swinging, advancing or retreating creature, attacking, again and again, with its sword it brought, hidden under its cape, to the labyrinth to kill the Minotaur, and now, facing him and his innocence, it felt ashamed. The Minotaur danced, clapped and stamped around it. He danced his joy of no longer being alone, he danced his hope of meeting the other Minotaurs, the girls and creatures who were like the one he was dancing with now. He forgot the sun while dancing, he forgot the curse. He was but cheerful, light, friendly, tender. He danced, and the creature lurked and jumped around the Minotaur, and when the sun was setting, their reflections became visible through the sun's thousandfold reflections. The Minotaur danced, happy to have found the Minotaurs and the new creatures, soon he would find the girl he'd taken, the girl who'd become lifeless and then left, and the other girls who'd been taken by Minotaurs and had become lifeless and left. The two danced towards each other and danced away from each other, the reflections met, covered themselves, shot through themselves. Everywhere, a Minotaur danced around, spun around, and everywhere the boy leaped out and back, recoiling, then bounded, poised to strike, and as the sun was setting

hinter dem Labyrinth versank und die Wände tiefrot aufleuchteten, stieß er zu, sprang zurück, lehnte sich an eine Wand, starrte auf den Minotaurus. Der machte noch einige Tanzschritte, das Schwert in der Brust, blieb stehen, zog sich mit der rechten Hand das Schwert heraus, betrachtete es verwundert, griff mit der linken Hand nach der Brust, aus der es schwarz herausquoll, warf das Schwert von sich, so daß es über den Boden schlitterte, preßte auch die rechte Hand vor die Brust, wankte, schien taumeln zu wollen, stand wieder unbeweglich. Er war verwirrt. Er begriff nicht, was seine Hände verfärbte, und nicht den Schmerz, der in seiner Brust wütete. Er fühlte nur, daß dieses Wesen, das ihn angesprungen und etwas in seinen Leib gestoßen hatte, ihn nicht liebte, wie ihn vorher alle geliebt hatten, die Minotauren, das Mädchen, die Mädchen, und wie er das fühlte, wurde er mißtrauisch, um so mehr als er nicht denken konnte, zog doch alles als Bilder in seinem Geiste vorüber und nicht in Begriffen, als ob er in einer Art Bilderschrift fühlte: Vielleicht hatte ihn das Mädchen gar nicht geliebt, und auch die anderen Mädchen hatten die Minotauren nicht geliebt, darum hatten sie sich unbeweglich gestellt und waren fortgegangen. Vielleicht gehörten sie dem neuen Wesen, das ähnlich wie das Mädchen aussah und doch anders, mit einem Leib, fast so kräftig wie der seine, und das ihn angesprungen hatte, wie die anderen neuen Wesen die Minotauren angesprungen hatten, die nun wie er die Hände auf ihre Brust preßten, aus der es schwarz herausquoll; und wie die sechs anderen Mädchen und die sechs anderen Jünglinge erschienen, einander die Hände reichend, so daß in den Spiegeln die Reihe der Herumirrenden nicht abzubrechen schien, sich vielmehr im Lichte des mächtigen Abends verdoppelte, vervierfachte, vervielfachte, und wie sie den Gefährten fanden, der an eine Wand lehnte und hoffte, der Minotaurus würde endlich zusammenbrechen,

beyond the labyrinth, and the walls were lighting
up in a deep red, he struck, jumped back,
leaned against a wall, stared at the
Minotaur, who made a few last dancing
steps with the sword in his chest, stopped,
pulled out the sword with his right
hand, startled, looked at it, with his left
hand grabbed his chest, from which
blackness oozed, tossed the sword away
from him, so that it slid across the ground,
pressed his right hand, too, against his chest,
stumbled, seemed to fall, and stood again,
fixed. He was confused. He didn't understand
what was staining his hands and what caused
the raging pain in his chest. He only felt that
this creature had jumped on him and thrust
something into his body, that it didn't love
him the way the others had loved him, the
Minotaurs, the girl, the girls, and as he felt
this, he became suspicious, more so because
he was no longer able to think with all those
pictures of everything flashing through
his mind, not as ideas but as images, as if
he were feeling pictures: Maybe the girl hadn't
actually loved him, and the other girls hadn't
really loved the Minotaurs, that's why they'd
acted lifeless and left. Maybe they belonged
to this new creature that looked like the girl,
but then again didn't, with a body almost as strong
as his, that had jumped him, just like the other new
creatures that had jumped the other Minotaurs who,
like him, pressed their hands against their chests
that oozed blackness; and as the six other girls
and the six other boys appeared, reaching
for each other's hands, so as not to break
the never-ending chain of lost beings
in the mirrors, the chain that doubled
in the light of this powerful evening, quadrupled,
and as they found the fellow who was leaning
against a wall and hoping the Minotaur
would finally collapse, the bull-man felt—

kam es dem Stiermenschen vor
—hätte er den Begriff gehabt—, die ganze
Menschheit bräche über ihn herein, ihn zu vernichten.
Er duckte sich. Er fühlte sich bedroht, und um
sich nicht zu fürchten, setzte er seiner Furcht
den Stolz entgegen, den Stolz, Minotaurus zu sein,
und was nicht Minotaurus war, war sein Feind.
Nur die Minotauren hatten das Recht,
im Labyrinth zu sein, in einer Welt, außer der es
für ihn keine Welt gab—mottete doch nur
ein vages Gefühl von Kuhwärme von den Ställen
her, wo er aufgewachsen war, in seiner Erinnerung.
Der Haß kam über ihn, den das Tier gegen den
Menschen hegt, von dem das Tier gezähmt,
mißbraucht, gejagt, geschlachtet, gefressen wird,
der Urhaß, der in jedem Tier glimmt. Seine Augen
wurden voll Wut. Aus seinem Maul trat Schaum,
und wie der Jüngling sich von der Wand löste,
weil er das Sich-Ducken des Minotaurus als dessen
Sterben mißdeutete, überzeugt, ihn tödlich
verwundet zu haben, und wie nun die Menschen,
die Mädchen und die Jünglinge, um den Geduckten,
dessen Wut sie nicht bemerkten, einen Kreis
bildeten und ebenfalls jubelten und im wilden
Ringelreigen um den Minotaurus herumtanzten,
immer schneller, immer übermütiger, als wären
sie gerettet, immer toller, ohne zu bedenken,
daß sie schon allein durch das Labyrinth verloren
waren—hätten sie doch auch beim Tode des
Stiermenschen den Ausgang aus den ineinandergeschachtelten
Spiegelwänden nicht gefunden—,
immer unvorsichtiger im Rausch ihrer vermeintlichen
Freiheit, immer enger den johlenden Kreis
ziehend, immer bedrohlicher in der hereinbrechenden
Nacht, in der er nur noch Menschen sah
und nicht mehr seine eigenen Spiegelbilder,
da die herumwirbelnden und herumhopsenden
Menschen ihm die Sicht auf die Wände des Labyrinths
verdeckten, so daß diese ihn nicht mehr
widerzuspiegeln vermochten, fühlte sich der
Minotaurus auch von den Minotauren im Stich

had he had the notion—as if all mankind were falling over him, to destroy him. He crouched. He felt threatened, and in order to not be afraid, he set his fear against his pride, the pride of being a Minotaur, and whatever wasn't a Minotaur was his enemy. Only Minotaurs had the right to be in the labyrinth, the only world that existed for him—even though in his memory the faint sensation of bovine warmth came in from the stable where he grew up. Hate came over him, the hate an animal harbors against the man who tamed it, abused it, hunted it, slaughtered it, ate it, the primal hate that smolders in every animal. His eyes filled with rage. He foamed at the mouth, and as the boy broke away from the wall because he'd misjudged the Minotaur's crouching as its death, convinced that he'd fatally wounded it, and as the humans, the girls and the boys, not noticing its rage, formed a circle around the crouching beast and cheered while dancing wildly around the Minotaur, ever faster, ever more excited, as if they were saved, ever madder, without thinking that they were already lost in the labyrinth—even at the death of the bull-man they never would have found their way out of the intertwining glass walls—ever more careless in their supposed freedom, drawing the jeering circle smaller and smaller, ever more threatening in the falling light, where he saw only humans and no longer his own reflection, for the spinning around and jumping around humans blocked his view of the labyrinth's walls, so that they could not reflect his image any longer, and the Minotaur felt abandoned

gelassen und verraten. Er rollte die Augen, schnaubte, ging tiefer, spannte die Muskeln, schnellte hoch, rannte an, nahm ein Mädchen auf die Hörner und verschwand mit ihm, es immer wieder hochschleudernd, im Labyrinth. Darauf, wutschnaubend zurückkehrend, mit blutverschmierten Hörnern—so oft hatte er zugestoßen—, fand er die Menschen eng in einem schattenhaften Knäuel zusammengedrängt, während sich über ihnen der hungrige Gefiederdschungel auf den Wänden schon niedergelassen hatte, ein dunkles Knäuel über einem dunklen Knäuel, ein Geramsel, dessen Krächzen, Pfeifen, heiseres Schreien und Schnattern sich mit dem Angstgeheul der Menschen vermischte. Der Mond war irgendwo hinter dem Labyrinth am Aufgehen, die Nacht, nur spärlich von der versunkenen Sonne getönt, erhellte sich. Der Minotaurus griff an, stieß zu, in ein weiches Durcheinander von weißen Leibern, wühlte sich durch, stieß wieder zu, wälzte sich, trampelte herum, stampfte nieder, spießte auf, zerfetzte, schlug zu, zerschlitzte, während es um ihn herum niederstürzte, hackte, knackte, knirschte, riß, schmatzte, so daß der schreiende und heulende Menschenknäuel, in welchem der Minotaurus wütete, von einem dichten Geflatter kreischender Aasvögel eingehüllt wurde: Bartgeier, Schmutzgeier, Schopfgeier, Königsgeier, Kappen-, Kutten-, Ohren-, Kahlkopf- und Rabengeier, Kondor und Urubu schnappten, würgten hinunter, tauchten erneut hinein; ohne Unterlaß zustoßend, riß der wütende Stiermensch im Menschendurcheinander und -übereinander Glieder aus, soff Blut, brach Knochen, wühlte in Bäuchen und Schößen, bis die struppige Wolke von Flügeln, Federn, Hälsen, Augen, Schnäbeln, Fängen und Krallen im Mondlicht sich aufgelöst hatte. Der Minotaurus war allein. Geblendet vom Mond, sah er auf den kalten Wänden seine Spiegelbilder wieder als schwarze Schatten, die sich ineinanderschoben und

and betrayed by the other Minotaurs.
He rolled his eyes, snorted, lowered himself,
flexed his muscles, shot up, ran, gored
a girl and disappeared with her, hurling
her continuously, into the labyrinth.
After that, snorting angrily, returning
with blood smeared horns—so often
had he struck—he found the humans
tightly huddled together in a shadowy
ball, while the hungry jungle of feathers
had already lowered itself onto the walls,
a dark ball over a dark ball, all crammed
together, whose croaking, whistling, hoarse
screams and cackles blended with the terrified
cries of the humans. The moon was coming
up somewhere beyond the labyrinth, the night,
scarcely tinted by the color of the sunken sun,
lit up. The Minotaur attacked, struck the soft
mess of white bodies, burrowed through
it, struck again, wallowed in it, trampled
around, stumped down, gored, shredded,
hit, slashed while it collapsed all around him,
hacked, cracked, gritted, tore and smacked
around, so that the screaming and howling
human ball the Minotaur raged through
was shrouded by a dense flutter of chattering
vultures: Bearded vulture, Egyptian vulture,
Turkey vulture, King vulture, Hooded, Black,
Lappet-faced, White-headed, long-crested,
condor and urubu, snapped, gulped down,
dove into it anew; striking incessantly, the
raging bull-man tore out limbs from the
human mess, guzzled blood, broke bones,
burrowed in bellies and laps, until the bristly
cloud of wings, feathers, necks, eyes, beaks,
claws and talons had dissipated in the moonlight.
The Minotaur was alone. Blinded by the moon,
he saw his reflections again as black shadows
on the cold walls that slid into themselves
and grew together into a labyrinth of shadows
within the labyrinth. He lifted his arms,

zusammenwuchsen zu einem Schattenlabyrinth im Labyrinth. Er hob die Arme, drohte mit den Fäusten, schüttelte sie, mit ihm hoben seine Spiegelbilder die Arme, drohten mit den Fäusten, schüttelten sie, was seine Wut derart steigerte, daß er sich mit gesenktem Stierkopf blindlings dem ersten Schatten entgegenwarf. Er durchbrach die Wand, suchte wütend in den Glassplittern das Spiegelbild, das doch das seine war, es schien ihm unter den Splittern begraben zu sein. Er stieß mit dem gewaltigen Kopf zu, und als er an der nächsten Wand sein Spiegelbild erblickte, begriff er immer noch nicht, griff es erneut aufbrüllend an, warf sich ihm kopfvoran entgegen, so wie es sich ihm kopfvoran entgegenzuwerfen schien. Er prallte zurück, glotzte mit wütenden rötlichen Auerochsenaugen nach seinem Spiegelbild, das ihn wie er mit wütenden rötlichen Auerochsenaugen anglotzte. Er rannte wieder an, noch heftiger, prallte noch heftiger zurück, kam auf den Rücken zu liegen. Der Mond war immer noch hinter dem Labyrinth, aber er schien durch die Wände, sich in ihnen als Fast-Vollmond wiederspiegelnd, die Zacken der Krater seiner noch nicht gerundeten Seite grotesk vergrößert, und so oft spiegelte sich der Mond, daß der Minotaurus in ein Universum aus Stein zu blicken glaubte, das von Narben durchzogen war. Auf diese Mondwelt starrend, fürchtete er, sein Feind habe sich erhoben. Er rollte sich auf den Bauch, der Verräter hatte sich zwar nicht erhoben, aber lauerte auch auf dem Bauch zu ihm herüber. Der Minotaurus rutschte seinem Spiegelbild entgegen, das sich ihm auf die gleiche Weise näherte, er war bereit, aufzuschnellen und sich über den andern zu werfen, aber indem er den andern beobachtete, spürte er, wollte er aufschnellen, die gleiche Absicht in den Augen des andern. Er prägte sich das Gesicht des Verräters ein, pelzbedeckt, die breite Stirn von verfilzten Wollhaaren überwuchert, überhauft von einem Berg von Glassplittern,

threatened with his fists, shook them,
with him his reflections lifted their arms,
threatened with their fists, shook them,
which made his rage so intense, he threw
himself, head down and blind, against the
first shadow. He broke through the wall
and searched furiously for his reflection
amongst the broken bits of glass, the reflection
that seemed buried beneath the shattered glass.
He struck again with his giant head,
and when he saw his reflection
on the next wall, he still didn't get
it, attacked it again, roaring, threw
himself head first against it, thinking
his reflection was doing the same. He
bounced back, searched with raging
red aurochs's eyes for his reflection that,
like him, looked at him with raging red
aurochs's eyes. Again, he ran against it,
harder, bounced back even harder,
landed on his back. The moon was
still beyond the labyrinth, but it shone
through the walls, reflecting itself almost
as a full moon, grotesquely magnifying
the craters' jags of its yet to be rounded
side, and the moon was being reflected
so often, the Minotaur believed he was
looking into a universe of stone crossed
by scars. Looking at this moon-world,
he was afraid his enemy had gotten up.
He rolled onto his stomach, the traitor,
though, hadn't gotten up, he, too, was
lurking on his stomach, on the ground
before him. The Minotaur skidded towards
his reflection, which did the same, he was ready
to jump up and throw himself on top of the other,
but by watching the other, he felt the same
urge to jump in the other's eyes. He
memorized the other's face, coat, the broad
forehead overgrown with matted wool,
covered by a mountain of broken glass

die im Mondlicht bläulich funkelten, die kurzen
gebogenen Hörner, der sanft geneigte Nasenrücken,
das nasse Flotzmaul, die lange bläulichrote Zunge.
Der Minotaurus keuchte, so daß der Dampf
seiner Nüstern den Spiegel beschlug, dem er sich
entgegenschob, worauf er sein Spiegelbild nicht
mehr sah, strich, den Nebel zu verscheuchen,
unwillkürlich mit der Hand über die Nässe, und
überrascht, als hinter der glatten kalten Fläche das
riesige Stierengesicht des Verräters unvermittelt
auftauchte, schmetterte er mit der Stirn instinktiv zu,
schlug mit ihr an die Wand statt auf die Stirn des
andern, die in der Wand war und nicht außerhalb.
Er stutzte. Er nahm von der Wand Abstand,
funkelte sein Spiegelbild hasserfüllt an, und es ihn,
schlug mit der rechten Faust zu, das Spiegelbild
mit der linken, die beiden Fäuste trafen sich,
erneuter Schlagwechsel mit dem gleichen Ergebnis,
darauf schlug er mit beiden Fäusten zu, das Spiegelbild
ebenfalls, schließlich trommelte er an die Wand.
Er trommelte seine Wut, er trommelte seine
Gier zu zerstören, er trommelte seinen Wunsch
sich zu rächen, er trommelte seine Lust zu töten,
er trommelte seine Furcht, er trommelte seine
Rebellion, er trommelte seine Selbstbehauptung,
aber auf einmal spürte er, daß dieses Wesen vor
ihm, das ein Wesen wie er und dennoch sein
Verräter war, weil es ein anderes war und weil alles
sein Feind war, was nicht er war, nicht zu fassen
war, unangreifbar war. Zwar hatter er gleich
zu Beginn seines Erwachens im Labyrinth—
von dem er noch immer nicht wußte, daß es ein
Labyrinth war—gefühlt, daß zwischen ihm und den
Minotauren etwas Geheimnisvolles lag, etwas
Wandähnliches, aber da er mit ihnen dahingetanzt
hatte wie ihr Anführer, wie ihr König, wie ihr
Gott, dahin durch das Weltall der Minotauren,
hatte er nicht darauf geachtet, aber jetzt, nachdem
er das Mädchen genommen und seinen Leib an
den ihren und in ihren gepreßt hatte und nachdem
er die Leiber der anderen Menschen mit seinen

sparkling bluishly in the moonlight,
the short, crooked horns, softly sloped
bridge of the nose, the wet muzzle,
the long, bluish-red tongue. The Minotaur
panted and the steam from his nostrils
fogged over the mirror he was approaching,
whereupon he could no longer see his
reflection, he wiped his hand across
the wetness, spontaneously, to drive away
the fog and, surprised to see the traitor's
giant face appear behind the cold surface,
he bashed it instinctively with his forehead,
hit the wall instead of the other's forehead
that was in the wall, not outside of it. He was
startled. He stepped away, flashed his hate-filled
eyes at his reflection, and it at him,
hit it with his right fist, the reflection
with its left, and both fists met, a fresh
exchange of blows with the same result,
then he struck with both fists, the reflection
did the same, finally, he pounded the wall
with his fists. He pounded his rage, he pounded
his lust to destroy, he pounded his wish for
revenge, he pounded his desire to kill, he
pounded his fear, he pounded his rebellion,
he pounded his self-assertion, but all at once
he felt that the creature in front of him was
just like him, but a traitor at the same time,
because it was different, because it was
his enemy, anything that wasn't like him,
that couldn't be caught, that was
untouchable. Though he'd felt right
from the start, when he awoke in the labyrinth—
which he still didn't know was a labyrinth—
that there was something mysterious between
him and the other Minotaurs, something wall-like,
but because he'd danced around with
them like their leader, like a king, like their
god, through the universe of Minotaurs,
he hadn't paid attention, but now, after
he'd taken the girl and pressed his body

Hörnern durchstoßen und zerfetzt hatte, aus denen
es warm und rot herausgequollen war wie
aus seinem Leib, spürte er das Unwirkliche dieses
Wesens vor ihm, das ihn zwar verraten hatte,
aber auch voller Glassplitter war wie er, und
vielleicht war sein Gesicht auch blutverschmiert wie
das seines Verräters. Er betastete sein Gesicht,
betrachtete seine Hände, auch sein Gesicht war
blutverschmiert. Er beobachtete sein Spiegelbild
mißtrauisch, tat, als ob er es nicht beobachtete,
er fühlte, daß es etwas zu sein schien, was es nicht
war. Er war entsetzt und neugierig zugleich.
Er wich zurück, sein Spiegelbild ebenso, und
allmählich ging ihm auf, daß er sich selber sich
gegenüber befand. Er versuchte zu flüchten, doch
wohin er sich auch wandte, stets stand er sich selber
gegenüber, er war eingemauert von sich selber,
überall war er selber, endlos war er selber,
vom Labyrinth ins Unendliche widergespiegelt.
Er spürte, daß es nicht viele Minotauren gab,
sondern nur einen Minotaurus, daß es nur ein Wesen
gab, wie er eines war, ein anderes nicht vor ihm und
ein anderes nicht nach ihm, daß er der Vereinzelte
war, der zugleich Aus- und Eingeschlossene,
daß es seinetwegen das Labyrinth gab, und das nur,
weil er geboren war, weil es ein Wesen
wie ihn nicht geben durfte, der Grenze willen,
die zwischen Tier und Mensch und Mensch
und den Göttern gesetzt worden ist, damit die
Welt in Ordnung bleibe und nicht zum Labyrinth
werde und damit ins Chaos zurückfalle, aus dem
sie entstanden war; und wie er das spürte, als ein
Fühlen ohne Begreifen, als eine Erleuchtung
ohne Erkennen, nicht als eine Mensheneinsicht
durch Begriffe, sondern als eine Minotaureneinsicht
durch Bilder und durch Gefühle, brach er
zusammen, und wie er dalag, zusammengerollt,
wie er im Leib Pasiphaes zusammengerollt
gewesen war, träumte der Minotaurus, er sei
ein Mensch. Er träumte von Sprache, er träumte
von Brüderlichkeit, er träumte von Freundschaft,

onto and into hers, and after he'd gored
and shredded the other humans, from whose
bodies it oozed red and warm, just like from his
own, he felt how fake the creature before him
was that had betrayed him yet, like him, was full
of broken glass, and perhaps his own face
was smeared with blood like the traitor's.
He touched his face, looked at his hands, his
face, too, was smeared with blood. He watched
his reflection, suspiciously, acted as if he didn't
watch it, he sensed it wasn't what it seemed to be.
He was horrified and curious
at the same time. He moved back,
his reflection also, gradually he realized
that he stood in front of himself. He tried
to run, but no matter where he turned,
he always faced himself, he was walled in
by himself, he was everywhere, he was infinite,
eternally reflected by the labyrinth into infinity.
He felt there weren't many Minotaurs, there
was only one Minotaur, that there was only
one creature like him, no other creature was
before or after him, that he was the only
one who was at once locked out and locked
in, that the labyrinth existed because of him,
because of his birth only, because something
like him shouldn't exist, for the sake
of separation between man and beast
set by the gods to keep the world
in order and not let it turn into
a labyrinth, back into a state of chaos
from which it sprung; and as he felt
this, as a feeling without understanding,
as his enlightenment without cognition,
not as human insight through ideas
but as a Minotaur's enlightenment
through images and feelings, he collapsed,
and as he lay there, curled up, curled up as
once inside Pasiphae's body, the Minotaur
dreamt of being human. He dreamt of language,
he dreamt of brotherhood, he dreamt

er träumte von Geborgenheit, er träumte
von Liebe, von Nähe, von Wärme und wußte
zugleich, wie er träumte, daß er ein Unwesen
war, daß ihm nie die Sprache, nie die Brüderlichkeit,
nie die Freundschaft, nie die Liebe,
nie die Nähe, nie die Wärme zufallen würden,
er träumte, wie Menschen von Göttern träumen,
mit der Traurigkeit des Menschen der Mensch,
mit der Traurigkeit des Tieres der Minotaurus.
So fand ihn denn Ariadne schlafend vor. Sie kam
tanzend mit ihrem Wollknäuel, den sie abrollen ließ,
und tanzend, fast zärtlich, wickelte sie das Ende
des roten Fadens um seine Hörner, tanzte dem
Faden nach wieder hinaus, und als der Minotaurus
erwachte, in einem gläsernen Morgen, sah er
unzählige Male gespiegelt einen Minotauren
auf sich zukommen, die Augen auf den Wollfaden
geheftet, als sei er eine Blutspur. Zuerst dachte
der Minotaurus, es sei sein Spiegelbild,
auch wenn er immer noch nicht begriff, was ein
Spigelbild sei, aber dann erfaßte er, daß der
andere Minotaurus ihm entgegenschritt, während
er auf dem Boden lag. Das verwirrte ihn.
Der Minotaurus erhob sich und bemerkte nicht,
daß das Ende des roten Wollfadens um seine
Hörner gewickelt war. Der andere kam näher.
Der Minotaurus warf beide Arme hoch, der andere
ebenfalls, der Minotaurus wurde argwöhnisch,
der andere konnte doch sein Spiegelbild sein,
dann schien es ihm wieder, als habe der andere
Minotaurus seine Arme nicht gleichzeitig mit ihm
hochgeworfen, die Spiegelbilder taten es sonst
alle gleichzeitig, aber er konnte sich getäuscht
haben, da beide widergespiegelt waren und der
andere nun stehengeblieben war. Der Minotaurus
machte einen Tanzschritt, die Spiegelbilder
auch, doch dismal tanzten viele Spiegelbilder
verzögert, er konnte es deutlich bemerken.
Der Minotaurus stand wieder unbeweglich
und spähte nach dem anderen Minotaurus, der auch
unbeweglich stand. Der Minotaurus versuchte

of friendship, he dreamt of security, he
dreamt of love, of closeness, of warmth,
and knew at the same time that he was
a monster, that neither love, nor language,
nor brotherhood, nor friendship, nor love,
nor closeness, nor warmth would ever happen
to him, he dreamt, as men dream of gods, of man
with the sadness of men, of the Minotaur
with the sadness of animals. This is how Ariadne
found him sleeping. She came dancing with her
ball of wool, which she let unroll, and dancing,
almost tenderly, she wrapped the end of the red
thread around his horns, danced
along the thread out of the labyrinth,
and when the Minotaur awoke,
in a glassy morning, he saw, infinitely
reflected, a Minotaur walking towards him,
his eyes fixed firmly on the red thread
as if on a trail of blood. First the Minotaur
thought it was his own reflection, though
he still didn't understand what a reflection
was, but then he realized that the other
Minotaur walked towards him while he
still lay on the ground. This baffled him.
The Minotaur stood up but didn't notice
the red thread whose end was wrapped
around his horns. The other one came
closer. The Minotaur threw both of his arms
in the air, the other one did the same,
the Minotaur became leery, the other
one could've been his own reflection, then
it seemed again as if the other Minotaur
didn't throw up his hands simultaneously
with him, usually, the reflections did
everything at the same time, but he could've
been mistaken, for both were being reflected,
and the other stood still now. The Minotaur
made a dance step, the reflections, too, but
this time, many reflections danced with a slight
delay, he could notice it clearly. The Minotaur
stood still again and peered at the other

zu denken. Er bewegte den kleinen Finger der rechten Hand, sah scharf hin, bewegte den Finger noch einmal, der andere bewegte den kleinen Finger der rechten Hand, was den Minotaurus beunruhigte, er war unsicher, der andere schien den kleinen Finger an der falschen Hand bewegt zu haben. Der andere Minotaurus stand unmittelbar vor ihm, aber es konnte auch ein Spiegelbild des anderen Minotaurus sein oder ein Spiegelbild seines eigenen Spiegelbilds, es war vielleicht sogar mit Denken nicht auszumachen, der andere hatte, wenn es einen anderen gab, einen Kopf wie er und einen Leib wie er. Der Minotaurus bewegte die rechte Hand, nun bewegte der andere die linke Hand, fast gleichzeitig, aber vielleicht auch gleichzeitig; und wie der Minotaurus all den Möglichkeiten nachspürte, sah er plötzlich, daß am Leib des anderen Minotaurs oder am Leib des Spiegelbilds des anderen Minotaurs an der Lende ein Gegenstand geheftet war, etwas Pelzartiges, von dem der Minotaurus zwar nicht wußte, was es war, aber das ihm bewies, daß er einem anderen Minotaurus oder dessen Spiegelbild gegenüberstand. Der Minotaurus schrie auf, wenn es auch mehr ein Brüllen war als ein Schreien, ein langgezogenes Aufheulen, Aufmuhen und Aufjaulen vor Freude darüber, daß er nicht mehr der Vereinzelte war, der zugleich Aus- und Eingeschlossene, daß es einen zweiten Minotaurus gab, nicht nur sein Ich, sondern auch ein Du.
Der Minotaurus begann zu tanzen. Er tanzte den Tanz der Brüderlichkeit, den Tanz der Freundschaft, den Tanz der Geborgenheit, den Tanz der Liebe, den Tanz der Nähe, den Tanz der Wärme.
Er tanzte sein Glück, er tanzte seine Zweisamkeit, er tanzte seine Erlösung, er tanzte den Untergang des Labyrinths, das donnernde Versinken seiner Wände und Spiegel in die Erde, er tanzte die Freundschaft zwischen den Minotauren, Tieren, Menschen und Göttern, den roten Wollfaden um die Hörner gewunden, er umtanzte

Minotaur standing still. The Minotaur tried
to think. He moved the small finger on his right
hand, focused on the other Minotaur, moved
his finger again, the other one moved his right
small finger, which alarmed him, the other
seemed to have moved the finger on
the wrong hand. The other Minotaur
stood directly in front of him, but it
could've been a reflection of the other
Minotaur or a reflection of his own reflection,
perhaps it wasn't possible to think this through,
the other one, if there was another one, had
a head and body like him. The Minotaur moved
his right hand, now the other one
moved his left hand, almost simultaneously,
maybe simultaneously; and as
the Minotaur traced all the possibilities,
he suddenly saw that there was
something attached to the other
Minotaur's loin, or on the loin of
the other Minotaur's reflection,
something pelt-like, something he
didn't know, but that proved to him
that he was facing another Minotaur
or its reflection. The Minotaur cried
out, even though it was more of a
roar rather than a cry, a long howl,
a loud mooing and yelping of happiness
about him no longer being the only
one, the one who's both locked in
and locked out, about there being
a second Minotaur, not only his I,
but a you. The Minotaur began to dance.
He danced the dance of friendship,
the dance of security, the dance of love,
the dance of closeness, the dance
of warmth. He danced his luck, he danced
his togetherness, he danced his salvation,
he danced the fall of the labyrinth,
the thunderous sinking of his walls
and mirrors into the earth, he danced

den andern Minotaurus, der den roten Wollfaden
spannte und den Dolch aus der Scheide aus
Pelz zog, ohne daß der Minotaurus es bemerkte,
und die Spiegelbilder des einen umtanzten die
Spiegelbilder des andern, die einen roten Wollfaden
spannten und einen Dolch aus der Scheide aus
Pelz zogen, und als der Minotaurus in die geöffneten
Arme des andern stürzte, im Vertrauen darauf,
einen Freund gefunden zu haben, ein Wesen wie er,
und als seine Spiegelbilder in die Arme der
Spiegelbilder des andern stürzten, stieß der andere zu,
und seine Spiegelbilder stießen zu, und so sicher
senkte der andere den Dolch in den Rücken,
daß der Minotaurus schon tot war, als er
zu Boden sank. Theseus nahm die Stiermaske vom
Gesicht, und alle seine Spiegelbilder nahmen
die Stiermaske vom Gesicht, wickelte den roten
Wollfaden auf und verschwand aus dem Labyrinth,
und alle seine Spiegelbilder wickelten den
roten Wollfaden auf und verschwanden aus dem
Labyrinth, das nichts mehr widerspiegelte als
endlos den dunklen Kadaver des Minotaurus.
Dann, bevor die Sonne kam, kamen die Vögel.

the friendship between Minotaurs, animals,
men and gods, the red woolen thread
wrapped around his horns, he danced
around the other Minotaur, who stretched
the red thread and took the dagger from
its sheath made of pelt, and as
the Minotaur fell into the other's
open arms, trusting to have found
a friend, a creature like him, as his
reflections fell into the arms of the other's
reflections, the other struck, and its reflections
struck, and the other's dagger struck his back
so perfectly that the Minotaur was already
dead as he hit the ground. Theseus took
off his bull mask, and all of his
reflections took off their bull masks,
recoiled the red thread and disappeared
from the labyrinth, and all of his
reflections recoiled the red threads
and disappeared from the labyrinth
that no longer endlessly reflected anything
but the Minotaur's dark carcass. Then,
before the sun came, came the birds.

HYMNS AND CURSES

by Peter Rüedi

At the end of the 1970s, Friedrich Dürrenmatt began preparing his Collected Works. He had occupied himself with the history of his unwritten material since 1969, tracing the reasons that prevented them from being written, and consequently searching for the mysterious subject that reigned over the different I's of his written works. He drew his conclusions from his notion that the boundary between the finished and unfinished, the mastered and failed, and the seemingly completed and abandoned, is blurred. His engagement with the published work was a result of his work on the unpublished, both investigations of the reasons and limits of imagination and thought. What allowed different material to become pieces, what prevented their shape? The answer to this question could be comprised only of further questions. Just as the ending of a piece (prose or drama) was often only temporary—its material, which, even after the premier or printing of it, never let go of him— "the work" is altogether open and its reason obscure. It is pure possibility, and "the possible is monstrous." For the author, death, the only human certainty, is what completes the work; but in the minds of those who continue to deal with him, it is still in motion.

Dürrenmatt defined the shape of the *Collected Works* (1980) himself, the arrangement of plays, radio plays, prose, and essays (the critical and theoretical works on theatre, literature, fine arts, politics, natural science, and philosophy). Yet we cannot find a volume of collected poems. When they do appear, however, sparingly interspersed, from Volumes 24 and 26 to 28, between essays, monologues, and reflections, almost as if Dürrenmatt wanted to neutralize them within the thematic context, it is deliberate. He never saw himself as a poet.

Aside from the fact that not every poem is necessarily lyric and not every play dramatic, the young Dürrenmatt of *It Is Written* and *The Blind One* could easily be seen as a lyric playwright (as well as an epic one in some of his major works); furthermore, even though there are mostly other subjects that reign over the so-called "lyric I" in his relatively few poems, and despite his self-assessment, the selection in this present volume offers rare moments of another, lyric Dürrenmatt. Still, why didn't he recognize himself as such?

The poem refers to its author, the poet, if not the numinous entity that speaks through him. Since the early 1950s, Dürrenmatt insisted on the occupational title "writer." This was not hairsplitting, but routine: writing as trade, one aimed against consecrated artists, according to him most fully embodied by Stefan George. Throughout his life, Dürrenmatt felt himself fixed between a non-formalistic aesthetic "based on material" and an obsession with control, the need to keep filing at it, the furor of revision: "The possible is monstrous. / The addiction / to perfection / destroys most things. / What remains / are splinters / that have been filed at needlessly."

The formula of the "worst possible turn," distinctive enough in connection with *The Physicists*, the great hermetic exception in Dürrenmatt's drama of the open form, suggests finality, causal organization as the single possible ending. And as the countless variations of nearly all of his endings demonstrate, the formula is ambiguous (he understood the "worst possible turn" as nothing more than the moment in which a character turns portrayable). The material grew beyond the single work, beyond set deadlines of publication or premier, transforming itself and its often provisionally determined form. The pain of having to settle on a result corresponded to and contradicted his aversion to the perfect, the concluded, the hermetic. He was both fascinated and disturbed by the unfinished and fragmentary. He was interested in processes, not results.

Writing as a way of life: to seek as well as curse the resistance to the arduous trade. A few of the most beautiful poems in this short collection deal with the vain hope of deliverance from this torment caused by an involuntary compulsion for perfection and the call for the humility of resignation; futile, hence, because of the themes of these poems, including, among others, the momentary desire for fulfillment and the unquestionable identity of form and content. None of the few poems Dürrenmatt included in the 1980 edition—as if he was, albeit reluctantly, unable to deny their consideration—were filed at, unlike the plays.

There's a noteworthy entry in Dürrenmatt's 1950 day planner included in the *Nachlaß*: "I'm realizing that everything poetic must happen not skillfully but blindly. An adventure. Letting oneself drift from material to unknown destinations. What one learns eventually: the art of navigation. My damned vice in writing: the hyper-pedantry of my presentation. But perhaps the

necessary self-control lies behind all of this." Already identified here is the polarity between self-generating material and the need to do it justice, creatively. The "poetic" and "writing": it almost reads like "desire and the normal."

The cliché of the aura of pure feeling that prevails in a poem arose from the late-romantic understanding of the lyric as a kind of unrestrained, subjective authority on the one hand, and the greatest possible intimacy on the other. Yet it doesn't actually apply to lyric poetry, not to mention the art of the ballad, the didactic poems of the Baroque period, the mediaeval battle poems; it doesn't apply to the majority of verse in world literature. And it surely misses Dürrenmatt's poems, even though they will baffle anyone who sees the author as a "thought-smith," who knows him as a constructor of allegories and world-parables, or better: who has read Dürrenmatt's plays and novels primarily with an eye for structure.

One of Dürrenmatt's central concepts is "distance." He was fundamentally suspicious of subjectivity and intimacy. Distance is not only the premise of his entire oeuvre, it is a quality of life, removed from free will as an act of self-defense or moral imperative. ("Be human, step back.") His aesthetic is one of refused empathy and imitation. Which doesn't mean "insensitivity," or disdain for feelings, the "sphere of man, without which his knowledge and his will are in vain: not the sphere of man's truth or error, but the sphere of his truthfulness and dignity, as well as his joy and sorrow, his hope and despair, the immense sphere of his feelings" (*Neuchâtel Speech*, 1981). Dürrenmatt, however, was "skeptical of any confession, for subjective thought retains a certain pride in the face of objective thought—or shame—so that it doesn't respond to answers that can only be answered subjectively" (afterword to *The Accomplice*). Nevertheless, he's by no means being ironic when he concludes his last letter to Max Frisch with the following line: "As one who, like you, is so determined to make his case the world, I always saw you, who's equally stubborn to make his case the world, as a correction of my writing" (11 May 1986).

Intimacy and subjectivity, as well as his "I," in a sense, were not Dürrenmatt's "case"; neither was the hermeticism in a however-mannered classicism of a linguistic work of art. To make language absolute was very suspect to someone who was beset by images, an opinion he shared with the great Fritz Mauthner, who begins his comprehensive three-volume *Contributions to a Critique*

of Language with these memorable sentences: "'In the beginning was the Word.' With the Word, men stand at the beginning of their knowledge, but they stop still if they stick to the word. He who wishes to move on, even if it be only a tiny step that may serve to advance the thought efforts of an entire lifetime, he must try to redeem the world from the tyranny of language."

The most obvious among the poems in this collection are the ones written for plays. The ones selected were those that can be read independently of their dramaturgic function: *The Maqamat of Akki the Beggar* from *An Angel Comes to Babylon*, a few songs from *Frank V.*, *A Solomonic Psalm, to Be Sung to Astronauts* from *The Physicists*, the "Choir of the Immortals" from *The Deadline*, the "Song of the Marxs" from *Achterloo IV.* The maqam, an Arabic rhymed prose form, seems to initially disagree with Mauthner's admired language skepticism. "The Maqamat of Akki are nothing more than the outermost possibility of his language, and thus a versification of his character. Within them, Akki turns entirely into language, is language, has turned into language, and that's what a playwright must always strive for: that there are moments in his theatre when the characters he writes become language and nothing else" (*Problems of the Theatre*, 1954). His *Letter to Maria Becker* from 1967 revises this, however: "When I first began writing for the theatre"—a beginning that reaches as far back as the writing of *An Angel*—"an actor was a 'bearer of roles.' He had to recite my texts; the text was everything and the person a being that had to be completely depicted through language . . . I have lost this beautiful belief in the omnipotence of language. Because it is not true. Man is more than language, his silence is more powerful than his talk, or else he wouldn't be a mystery."

Admittedly, the maqamat in *An Angel* are not only a character's locution but, through the elevation into verse, a dramaturgic distancing tool, a rhetorical vehicle, a way to prevent realism. Many poems in this collection, not only the ones from plays, originated from a rhetorical stance. Hymns and curses: these too are, not just since the baroque period, possibilities of poetry.

In a 1979 lecture given in Poland, Bernhard Böschenstein, the Swiss Germanist, remembers his encounter with Dürrenmatt. Böschenstein was the godson of Wilhelm Steins, the art historian and Georgian, whose circle Dürrenmatt was associated with during his years as a student in Berne. The sixteen-year-old high school student and the twenty-seven-year-old author discussed

poetry: the teenager's own attempts, the work of Georg Trakl, whom Dürrenmatt admired (especially "Rondel," first published in Switzerland in the edition by Kurt Horwitz, who discovered Dürrenmatt), the lyrics of Gryphius, where, "as he said, feeling turns into reflection." Here, Böschenstein suspects an influence from Dürrenmatt's other mentor, Ernst Ginsberg, who loved to recite baroque poetry (Ginsberg published the selected works of Else Lasker-Schüler). Dürrenmatt loved Brecht's love poem from *Mahogany*, the poems of Claudius, the final chorus from the third act of *Faust II*: "This led to his preference for Goethe's baroque language in *Pandora*, which he suggested for my high school reading list in 1950 . . . Later I found out from Emil Steiger that Karl Kraus recommended the poems to his friend Horwitz, who introduced them to Dürrenmatt. Language as costume, as sensual quality, as word-matter, exposed to processes and now showing an autonomous splendor of word-building, detached from its own expression." Dürrenmatt's contribution to *Favorite Poems*, an anthology published by Artemis, points to the four-part choir from *Faust II* and Trakl's "Rondel."

When asked about genre, Dürrenmatt enjoyed using analogies drawn from sportive disciplines: novelists were long-distance-, playwrights medium-, and poets short-distance-runners or "sprinters." He didn't despise the sprinters at all; their distance wasn't "his case," even though he always yearned for their ease and speed, for the "Book of Poems while Smoking a Lunchtime Cigar," for "Poems written in one, two minutes, / in a daydream (the sun stood high), / lightning that illuminates our earthly darkness."

Such lightning, to him, was the poetry of Paul Celan. In *Turmbau* (*Tower Building*), from the second volume of *Stoffe* (*Material*), he goes as far as to say that "Only once I met Paul Celan in Paris did poems become important to me." A friendship developed, which was based on the respect for each other's differences. In Dürrenmatt's case, it was certainly the admiration for an art in which "associations pierced grammar, so to speak" (*Neuchâtel Speech*). In his work, undercurrents of the Bernese dialect pierced the surface of normative Modern High German grammar. There's a signed poem of Celan's, "Above Neuchâtel," dedicated to Lotti and Friedrich Dürrenmatt, from 2 August 1964, in the *Nachlaß*.

Celan did not influence Dürrenmatt's poems, nor are we able to detect traces of Trakl, Heyms, Lasker-Schüler, or Benn

(whom, despite their completely differing approaches, he admired). But when we say that Dürrenmatt was interested in everything but himself, we can say the same for his varied aesthetic positions—from Frisch to Benn.

Where the *I* has lost its naturalness and unquestionability, where, as Dürrenmatt says in his afterword to *The Accomplice*, it has become "fiction," it cannot speak as the absolute authority of the lyric poem; but then the question remains, "Who the hell is writing here?" Nevertheless, there are some stunning poems in this collection, where Dürrenmatt speaks as Dürrenmatt, a voice we can usually hear only in his later prose—pieces where he allows himself some sensitivity. There's even a love poem (one the cleverest circle of experts of literary guesswork would fail).

"There are empowering sentences / but they don't need to be / written down // Free your hand. // It's never about sentences. Only the / Work counts. / Fools criticize a sentence / Few see the whole thing." This is the other side of these poems. Even though they belong to "lightning," they are, in the sharply lit moment, part of the whole, interwoven with a work in which everything is connected to everything else. In the lapidary "View through the Window," the room expands from the nearest to the foreground, middle ground, and background, into infinity, from present to past: "Then stars, their light years old / Only the past." Dürrenmatt was still occupied by this thought in *Stoffe*: "Simultaneity doesn't say anything. The distant approached in time. Reality stretches gradually. Nothing happens without the background, where we find the reasons for writing and thinking, but this background is graded like a landscape . . . We are not surrounded by the past, but by pasts, by a world of interwoven and woven-through memories."

The connections to Dürrenmatt's oeuvre are even clearer in the reflective poems, which, in their reflection, concern themselves with the yearning for the pure (non-reflected) moment ("O ease of thought that turns to crime / when worked on!"). "God and Péguy," formally a monologue like the negative proof of God written, half a life later, in 1985, claims the ethics of a single person against the understanding of God via the state or a nationalistic ideology ("As if it didn't come down / to every single individual"), a text written from postwar experience to postwar-non-experience. Like the declaration of a bankrupt Western world in "To Europe." While "When I Walk through German Cities" picks up on the difficult relationship of the Swiss with their neighbors to the north, the

tension of an author's seizing of Swiss-German against "mankind's prime," a theme that would occupy Dürrenmatt until *Stoffe*. The text sets the stage for *Swiss Psalm I*, which, like the two subsequent pieces, expresses Dürrenmatt's love-hate relationship with the place "behind the moon."

At times there's a Brechtian tone in "Who Wants to Make the World a Place to Stay" and the songs from *Frank V*. Both are full of allusions to Dürrenmatt's own works ("Trapped in the collective / Shadowed by his neighbor, whom he already watches": and here it is again, the old motif of the early prose that renders even the speech for Václav Havel a scandal). And allusions to world literature: "We Rush to Our Ancestors" is a travesty of Matthias Claudius ("The Moon Has Risen"), just as the ending of the "Choir of the Immortals" from *The Deadline* is a travesty of the final chorus from *Faust II*. Finally, the beautiful farewell for Willy Birgel can be read as a prelude to Dürrenmatt's own goodbye to the theatre.

To provide an exhaustive commentary on the texts in this collection is impossible, and absurd, for it would need to be longer than the collection itself, and an interpretation of the ballads would finally stretch the boundaries completely. Dürrenmatt cut the ballad of Midas from *Midas or the Second Life*, the original title of the *King's Tragedy* published in 1991 by Diogenes (see references). "The Minotaur" corresponds to the text published in 1985. Both myths bear on the core of Dürrenmatt's work; on the one hand, the motif of the curse of mercy (*Greek Man Seeks Greek Wife*, but especially in *The Watchmaker*, as Dürrenmatt summarizes in the afterword to *An Angel Comes to Babylon*), on the other, the ambiguous, multi-layered, itself labyrinthine, complex of the labyrinth. So we read both texts as probes, as drills that reach deep beneath the foundation of Dürrenmatt's massif, exposing the layers of the whole. Here we should listen to the "Dramaturgic Advice," which is about much more than dramaturgy: "Don't give us any profound talk / Don't add to the mystery."

Translated by Daniele Pantano

EDITORS' NOTE

Friedrich Dürrenmatt began writing poems as early as 1942 and continued to do so in parallel with his work as playwright, author, and essayist. His poetry, however, appeared in the *feuilleton,* or literary sections of newspapers and magazines, which is customary in many European countries. The thirty-volume *Werkausgabe* (the *Collected Works*), published in collaboration with the author, included little more than a dozen poems—too few for a single volume and therefore interspersed throughout the individual volumes of essays. Dürrenmatt eventually added but one extra text: the ballad of "The Minotaur," which was published in 1985. The present volume contains a selection of the published and unpublished poems from Dürrenmatt's papers—the *Nachlaß*—as well as the songs and poems from his plays.

The scope of Dürrenmatt's lyric poetry became apparent only after his death. There are over sixty poems (mostly as typescript versions) in the folders, journals, notebooks, and manuscripts held at the Swiss Literary Archive in Berne, including the songs and poems Dürrenmatt himself extracted from his comedies, radio plays, and cabaret pieces. Short poems of a casual and indulgent nature are represented alongside the great ballads of his later work. Dürrenmatt's first lyric attempts date back to his years as a student in Berne and Zurich in the early 1940s, while the last poem at the Literary Archive stems from the year 1988.

Whenever he was asked about his literary beginnings, Dürrenmatt would emphasize, "In 1946 I became a writer." Consequently, the *Werkausgabe* begins with *It Is Written*, composed between 1945 and '46 and first staged in 1947; the prose work begins a little earlier (1942), albeit the author notes in his afterword that the first pieces were written "between 1942 and 1946"; the first of Dürrenmatt's essays included stems from 1950; and the earliest poem included is dated 1948.

The editors based the arrangement and organization of the present volume, first and foremost, on Dürrenmatt's own broadly formulated framework for the publication of his poetry: on the one hand, his own strict selection of poems for the *Werkausgabe* and his personal scope (which included, and can clearly be seen from his arrangement of the *Nachlaß*, the songs and poems from his plays), and on the other hand, the precise dating of his earliest

literary works. The present volume contains, therefore, in addition to the poems that are already part of the *Werkausgabe*, mainly selected songs and poems from the plays, a handful of previously unpublished pieces from the early 1950s and 1970s, the two great ballads from the late work—"The Minotaur" and "Midas"—as well as the poems from the *Nachlaß* that were first published in *Kant's Hope*. Dürrenmatt's thematic and contextual arrangement of the poems in the *Werkausgabe* has been adopted and the poems from the *Nachlaß* arranged and inserted accordingly.

REFERENCES

Gott und Péguy / God and Péguy (1948). From the *Werkausgabe in dreißig Bänden* (*Collected Works in Thirty Volumes*), published in collaboration with Dürrenmatt, Diogenes, Zurich, 1980 (hereinafter referred to as *WA*), Volume 27.

An Europa / To Europe (undated, ca. 1945–54). From the *Nachlaß* (*Personal Papers*). Various handwritten drafts and versions. The included text represents a fair copy of the last version.

Wenn ich durch die Städte Deutschlands gehe / When I Walk through German Cities (undated).
Typescript without title from the *Nachlaß*.

Schweizerpsalm I / Swiss Psalm I (1950). *Hortulus*, St. Gallen, Issue 48, 1960. From *WA*, Volume 28.

Schweizerpsalm II / Swiss Psalm II (1950). From *WA*, Volume 28.

Schweizerpsalm III / Swiss Psalm III (15 January 1971). From *WA*, Volume 28.

Wer die Erde wohnbar machen will / Who Wants to Make the World a Place to Stay (1963).
From *WA*, Volume 24 (untitled).

Wie Helden von Shakespeare / Like Shakespeare's Heroes (titled by original editor).

Poems and songs from *Opera of a Private Bank, Frank the Fifth* ("Like Shakespeare's Heroes" / "We Rush to Our Ancestors" / "What We Scam and Reap" / "Villains with Style Are Rare" / "Their Flesh and Blood" / "How the Situation Stands in Which We Are" / "The Resignation") (1958/59/64/80). From *WA*, Volume 6.

Ich habe ausgezeichnet gegessen / I Have Eaten an Excellent Meal. Johann Bockelson von Leyden's "Feast-Aria" from the play *It Is Written* (1945/46/47). From *WA*, Volume 1. Cut down to a few verses in the comedic version of *The Anabaptists* (1966/67), written twenty years later, it serves as the beginning of the monologue of King Bockelson on the throne (Part II, "14. King Bockelson," *WA*, Volume 10).

O Welt der Männer und der Morde / O World of Men and Murders. "Choir of the Immortals" from the comedy *The Deadline* (1975/76/revised version, 1980). From *WA*, Volume 15.

Midas / Midas (1983/84). The text of this ballad is based on two pages of the 8th version (14 May 1983) of *The King's Tragedy,*

or The Black Screen (the original title was *Midas, or The Second Life*). Originally included as "Midas's Ballad," this verse was eliminated on 6 April 1984 and re-written as an autonomous text. The included text represents a fair copy of the 6 April 1984 version with Dürrenmatt's own corrections, dated until 26 April 1984.

Für Willy Birgel / For Willy Birgel (1974). Poem in honor of Willy Birgel, Dürrenmatt's close friend and actor. Read by Wolfgang Stendar on Friday, 25 January 1974, during the commemoration in the Schauspielhaus, Zurich. From *Gesammelte Werke in sieben Bänden* (*Collected Works in Seven Volumes*), Volume 7, Diogenes, Zurich 1988, expanded reprint 1991).

Dramaturgischer Rat / Dramaturgic Advice (1961). From *WA*, Volume 24.

An Varlin / To Varlin (undated). Early versions titled *An Oskar Kokoschka / To Oskar Kokoschka.* From *WA*, Volume 26.

Gedichtband bei einer Mittagszigarre / Book of Poems while Smoking a Lunchtime Cigar (1950). From *WA,* Volume 26.

Vor uns hintastend, Liebes / Groping along, My Dear (undated, ca. 1970–74). From the *Nachlaß,* untitled. The included text represents the third and last handwritten version.

Kronenhalle / Kronenhalle (undated, early version titled *Mein Tisch / My Table,* ca. 1942/43). From *WA*, Volume 26.

Was soll an diesem Nachmittage / What's the Point This Afternoon (undated, ca. 1964/65). From the *Nachlaß,* untitled. The included text is the second and last handwritten version.

Vater mein, ein Riese steht im Wald / Father, My, There's a Giant in the Forest (undated, ca. 1957). From the *Nachlaß,* untitled. The included text represents the sixth and last handwritten version.

Meere / Seas (undated). From *WA,* Volume 26.

Spielregeln / Rules of the Game (undated). First captioned *Trost / Solace.* From *WA*, Volume 26.

Blick durchs Fenster / View through the Window (undated). Typescript from the *Nachlaß.*

Antares / Antares (1958). From *WA,* Volume 27.

Mond / Moon (1958). From *WA,* Volume 27.

Siriusbegleiter / Sirius's Companion (1958). First captioned *Weißer Zwerg / White Dwarf.* From *WA*, Volume 27.

Elektronische Hirne / Electric Brains (1958). From *WA,* Volume 27.

Ein Psalm Salomos, den Weltraumfahrern zu singen / A Solomonic Psalm, to Be Sung to Astronauts. Johan Wilhelm Möbius's poem

from the comedy *The Physicists* (1961/revised version, 1980). From WA, Volume 7.

Lied / Song (undated). First written as *"Beggar Akki's Song"* for the 1953 premier of the comedy *An Angel Comes to Babylon.* "Die Tat" / "The Act," Zurich, 1 August 1959. From *WA*, Volume 27.

Die Makamen des Bettlers Akki / The Maqamat of Akki the Beggar. From the fragmentary comedy *An Angel Comes to Babylon* (1953 revised edition, 1980). From *WA,* Volume 4.

Das Unvermeidliche wartet / The Inevitable Waits (undated). From *WA,* Volume 27.

Nur das Nichtige hat Bestand / Only Nothingness Stands (undated). From the *Nachlaß,* untitled. First published as *Wütend* (Angry) in *Kants Hoffnung* (Kant's Hope). *Zwei politische Reden und zwei Gedichte aus dem Nachlaß* (Two Political Speeches and Two Poems from the Nachlaß). *Mit einem Essay von Walter Jens* (With an Essay by Walter Jens), Diogenes, Zurich, 1991 (hereinafter referred to as K).

Ergreife die Feder müde / When you're Tired, Pick Up the Pen (undated). From the *Nachlaß,* untitled. From *K.*

Der Menschen Ketten loszuketten / To Unchain Man's Chains. "Lied der Marxe" / "Song of the Marxs," written for the premier of *Achterloo IV* (1988) at the 1988 Schwetzinger Festspiele. It was, however, deleted during rehearsals. The included text is a typescript from 5 May 1988.

Minotaurus / The Minotaur (1984/85). First captioned *Entwurf zu einem Ballett / Sketch for a Ballet.* Published as *Minotaurus. Eine Ballade. Mit Zeichnungen des Autors* (The Minotaur. A Ballad. With Drawings by the Author), Diogenes, Zurich, 1985.

The present volume is based on material located at the Swiss Literary Archives in Berne, Switzerland, an institution of the Swiss National Library and the Swiss Federal Office of Culture. The publishers and editors, as well as the translator, would like to thank the Swiss Literary Archives in Berne, especially Dr. Thomas Feitknecht for the unconditional access to the Dürrenmatt Archive, and Ueli Weber for his important advice and valuable assistance during the preparation of this book.

NOTES

Pages 14, 15: *Péguy, Charles* (1873–1914). French writer and publisher of the literary-political *Cahiers de la Quinzaine*, he enjoyed a tremendous intellectual influence over France on the eve of WWI; originally a socialist and Dreyfusist, he developed into an uncompromising champion of a Catholic-Mystic traditionalism and nationalism; he fell in the battle of the Marne. There's a handwritten note at the end of the typescript of "God and Péguy": "Shortly after the war, a Swiss newspaper published one of Péguy's poems: 'Gott und Frankreich' ('God and France'). The parody refers to this nationalistic-religious poem."

Pages 38, 39: *Westmoreland, William Childs* (1914–2005). U.S. Army General; 1964–68, commanded American military operations in Vietnam; 1968–72, U.S. Army Chief of Staff.

Pages 40, 41: *Napoleon Bonaparte* (1769–1821). Dürrenmatt propably meant the 1798 defeat of the Bernese troops at Fraubrunn and in the Grauholz.

Villard, Arthur (1917–1995). Teacher in Biel (Canton of Berne). Socialist politician; 1971–1979, member of the National Council. Although not a pacifist, he was a conscientious objector out of protest against the sentencing of conscientious objectors by the Swiss courts. In 1969, Dürrenmatt, after having received the Great Prize for Literature from the Canton of Berne, gave the prize money to Villard, Sergious Golowin, and Ignaz Vogel.

Pages 76, 77: *Fibonacci, Leonardo* (also known as N. Leonardo of Pisa and Leonardo Pisano; ca. 1170–ca. 1240). Italian mathematician and merchant.

Pages 104, 105: *Birgel, Willy* (1891–1973). German actor; started working for the Schauspielhaus Zurich in 1959, where he played many roles, including Koppe in *Der Meteor / The Meteor* (premiered in 1966), the Cardinal and Mathisson in *Die Wiedertäufer / The Anabaptists* (premiered in 1967), Erdgeist/Wagner/Frosch/böser Geist in *Urfaust* (premiered in 1970), and, finally, Jack in *Der Mitmacher / The Collaborator* (premiered in 1973).

Seyferth, Wilfried (1908–1954). German actor and director; after 1945, worked for, amongst others, the Schauspielhaus Zurich and the Munich Kammerspielhaus; played the role of Mönch in *Es steht geschrieben / It Is Written* (premiered in Zurich in 1974) as well as Saint-Claude *in Die Ehe des Herrn Mississippi / The Marriage of Mr. Mississippi* (premiered in Zurich in 1952).

Kalser, Erwin (1883–1958). German actor, immigrated to Switzerland in 1933, played at the Stadttheater Basel and at the Schauspielhaus Zurich from 1933– 39 and 1946–52; played the Bishop in the premiere of *Es steht geschrieben / It Is Written* (Zurich 1947) and the title role in *Romulus der Große / Romulus the Great* (Zurich 1949).

Graf, Robert (1923–1966). German actor; Munich Kammerspiele from 1951–66.

Teege, Joachim (1925–1969). German actor; played the role of Einstein in *Die Physiker / The Physicists* (Frankfurt 1962).

Domin, Friedrich (1902–1961). German actor; played the title role in *Die Ehe des Herrn Mississippi* (premiered at the Munich Kammerspiele in 1962).

Carlsen, Traute (1887–1968). German actress. Immigrated, via Vienna, to Switzerland in 1933. Worked at the Schauspielhaus Zurich. As an eighty-year-old, played Roede, the old actress, in *Die Widertäufer / The Anabaptists* (premiered in Zurich in 1967); Dürrenmatt's notes: "I wrote the part in honor of Traute Carlsen. She'd just turned eighty, and there were no roles for her to play. So I wrote one for her. She was very happy, and I happier, because it upset the critic I loved to annoy the most."

Ginsberg, Ernst (1904–1964). German actor, director, and writer; immigrated, via Vienna, to Switzerland in 1933; worked in Zurich and played the role of Übelohe in *Die Ehe des Herrn Mississippi / The Marriage of Mr. Mississippi* (premiered, 2nd version, Zurich in 1957); also worked as the director of the Basler Stadttheater, where he staged the premiers of *Der Blinde / The Blind Man* in 1948 and *Romulus der Große / Romulus the Great* in 1949; is considered, along with Kurt Horowitz, Dürrenmatt's discoverer and mentor.

Steckel, Leonard (1901–1971). German actor. Immigrated to Switzerland in 1933, where he worked as an actor and director. Directed the premier of *Herkules und der Stall des Augias / Hercules and the Augian Stable* (Zurich 1966), played Schwitter in *Der Meteor / The Meteor* (premiered in Zurich in 1966). He died in a train crash.

Pages 110, 111: *Varlin* (actually Willy Guggenheim; 1900–1977). Swiss painter, who on many occasions painted Dürrenmatt as well as their mutual friend, the novelist and publisher, Hugo Loetscher (1929–2009).

Pages 120, 121: *Zumsteg, Hulda* (1890–1984). Owner of the *Kronenhalle*, Dürrenmatt's favorite restaurant in Zurich.

Giehse, Therese (1898–1975). German actress. Immigrated to Switzerland in 1933. Played the title role in *Der Besuch der alten Dame / The Visit* (premiered in Zurich in 1956), Ottilie, on stage and on screen, in *Frank V. / Frank the Fifth* (premiered in Zurich in 1959; film version in 1967), and the mad doctor Mathilde von Zahnd in *Die Physiker / The Physicists* (premiered in Zurich in 1962).

Pages 155, 156: *Gody*. Unclear reference. Usually viewed as a combination of God, Godot, the eponymous hero of Samuel Beckett's *Waiting for Godot*, and Gody Suter (longtime fiction editor at the *Zürcher Weltwoche*; 1919–1984).

Pages 68, 69 and 102, 103: Words and letters marked by brackets refer to uncertain passages in Dürrenmatt's original, handwritten or typed, versions.

ABOUT THE AUTHOR

Friedrich Dürrenmatt (1921–1990) is universally recognized as the most prominent Swiss novelist, playwright, and essayist of the twentieth century and as one of the most influential authors of modern literature. Dürrenmatt's works have been translated into virtually all languages, and his oeuvre is inextricably linked to the modernist canon. Among his best-known works are the plays *The Visit* (1956) and *The Physicists* (1962), as well as the novels *The Judge and His Executioner* (1952) and *The Pledge* (1958). In 2001, *The Pledge* was adapted for the screen (directed by Sean Penn and starring Jack Nicholson).

ABOUT THE TRANSLATOR

Daniele Pantano is a Swiss poet, translator, critic, and editor born of Sicilian and German parentage in Langenthal (Canton of Berne). Pantano has taught at the University of South Florida and served as the Visiting Poet-in-Residence at Florida Southern College. He divides his time between Switzerland, the United States, and England, where he's Senior Lecturer in Creative Writing at Edge Hill University. For more information, please visit www.danielepantano.ch.

INDEX OF TITLES AND FIRST LINES IN ENGLISH

Page numbers refer to the text; those in italics, following poem titles, point to the references.

INDEX OF TITLES AND FIRST LINES IN GERMAN

Page numbers refer to the text; those in italics, following poem titles, point to the references.